Express Guide

Red Hat

Enterprise Linux

Centos

Version 8

Shiv Kumar Goyal

Preface

This book is specially for system administrators or Linux enthusiast. This book is written in such manner that it covers practical aspects of RedHat Enterprise Linux and centos. If you are plaining to deploy version 8 of Redhat Enterprise Linux or maintaining it than this book is for you. All procedures written in the book are to the point with available screen shots and output samples. If you are short of time and hates reading bulky books, then this book is for you. It covers all articles from basics to advance level.

I hope you will like this book

Thanks

Shiv Kumar Goyal

Table of Contents

INTRODUCTION...1

NEW FEATURES IN RED HAT ENTERPRISE LINUX VERSION 8.....................................5

MINIMUM SYSTEM REQUIREMENT..7

INSTALLATION...8

CONNECTING YOUR PC TO RHEL SERVER 26

NETWORK 28

USERS MANAGEMENT 45

SOFTWARE MANAGEMENT 60

MANAGING SERVICES 87

OPENSSH..96

VNC..104

WEB SERVER 107

EXPLORING SHELL 115

BACKUP AND RESTORE 121

ARCHIVING AND COMPRESSION 130

FIREWALL...135

PARTITION 145

FILE SYSTEM 159

SWAP SPACE 163

LOGICAL VOLUME MANAGER 166

NFS 177

LVM SNAPSHOT 180

UTILITIES AND COMMANDS 182

PIPING AND REDIRECTION 189

PROCESS AND THREADS 193

AUTOMATING TASKS 197

BOOT PROCESS 200

LOG MANAGEMENT 202

SELINUX 213

SYSTEM MONITORING TOOLS 217

COCKPIT 223

Chapter 1.

Introduction

An operating system is piece of software, which manages hardware resources on your computer. Operating System is a layer that runs in between your applications and hardware. To run any application, you require operating system on your machine. There are lot of operating system available in the market like MS windows, Apple Mac OS, Unix, Linux etc. Just like Windows 7, MS Windows 10 and Mac OS, Linux is a prominent operating system. Unlike other OS, Linux is an open source operating system that means source code is freely available. The benefit of having open source is that anyone can see the source code and modify it according to his own requirements.

In 1991 Linus Torvalds started Linux project. Linux was originally developed for Intel based personal computers but eventually it had been ported to other platforms. Not only on PC, Linux kernel is also used in Android Operating system on your smartphones. As Linux is open source project lot of companies and individual used this source code and started creating their own Linux distributions. Today there are thousands of Linux distributions in the market, but some distributions enjoy lion share among the Linux users. Over the time lot of Linux communities and companies use these popular distributions as base to create their own distribution flavor by modifying or adding some packages. Broadly, we can classify Linux distribution based on their source distribution for example Centos, Oracle and Scientific Linux are based on Redhat whereas Debian based distributions are Ubuntu, Mint, tails and PureOS etc.

Free V/s Paid

Linux although is open source project but there are two types of Linux distribution available one is free and other is paid. Free is self-explanatory you do not have to pay anything. If you have any problem, you can take help of volunteers working for that Linux community. However, problem is that this type of support is not time bond as it is voluntarily. For corporate sector where Linux is used in production environment, this is not acceptable. So companies who uses mission critical Linux servers and computers prefers paid type of Linux Distribution where they pay fixed amount as subscription and support fee to get services with Service Level Agreement (SLA). These paid Linux distribution companies keeps team of Linux experts to provide support and fixes.

The prominent players in free Linux are Ubuntu, Debian, Fedora, Centos, Opensuse etc. Red hat and SUSE are major players in non-free enterprise Linux distribution.

Relationship between Fedora and Red Hat Enterprise Linux

Both the Fedora Linux and Red Hat Enterprise Linux are open source technologies. Fedora although supported by Red Hat company but still it is community project built by the community. On other hand Red Hat Enterprise Linux is developed by Red Hat company. Fedora is community project focused on the individuals who wants to try and use bleeding edge technology. Fedora releases new version after every six months and provide updates support for 13 months where as new version of Red Hat comes out every few years and supported for 10 Years or more. Therefore, Red Hat Enterprise Linux is first choice for Enterprise IT platform where stability and long term release is primary requirement.

What is community Project?

Linux community projects are those projects in which Linux enthusiast and contributors come together to build a project which helps in exploring new technologies and solutions. Contributor can be an end user, developer or tester or even designer. These type of projects are generally built voluntarily. But still to run these type of project you require financial power for the infrastructure like websites ,servers and office. Some communities take help from individuals as donation on other hand some projects get sponsorship from corporate companies like RedHat, IBM, HP etc. In return these companies take advantage of the new technologies developed by these communities. Like in the case of Fedora project which is sponsored by RedHat. The developers of both distributions collaborate together in fixing bugs and improving the technologies developed by Fedora community.

Centos and Red hat Linux

Red Hat Enterprise Linux is known for its stability. As name suggest it is enterprise level Linux. The Centos (short for **C**ommunity **ENT**erprise **O**perating **S**ystem) Linux distribution is free Linux distribution derived from source code of Red hat Enterprise Linux. It is enterprise class Linux distribution. Unlike Red Hat where you have to pay subscription fee for updates and upgrades, Centos is fully free. Centos Linux provides same software packages as Red hat but without support from Red hat. Centos takes source code from Red Hat repositories. Using this source code Centos rebrand it after removing Red Hat logos, trademarks and proprietary software. Centos also removes and modify some original software provided by Red Hat like subscription manager, which is not required in Centos.

## Chapter 2

New Features in Red Hat Enterprise Linux Version 8

Red Hat Enterprise Linux distribution is a stable platform derived from the sources of Fedora 28. With new version 8, RHEL has brought many improvements from its previous versions. Here is a summary of new features came with RHEL version 8:-

- The Cockpit is now available by default
- GNOME Shell version 3.28
- DNF as package management tool. For backward compatibility Yum is still working using DNF infrastructure.
- RPM v4.14 is distributed in RHEL 8. RPM now validates the whole package contents before starting the installation.
- RHEL 8 divided in to two main repositories BaseOS and Application Stream (AppStream).
- Higher memory support, up to 4PB of physical memory.
- instead of the Xorg server Wayland is default display server.
- XFS now supports shared copy-on-write data extent functionality
- Maximum XFS file system size is 1024 TiB in earlier version it was 500 TiB
- nftables replaces iptables as the default network filtering framework
- Python 3.6 is the default Python version
- PHP 7.2
- RHEL 8 provides Node.js 10. Previously Node.js was available only as Software Collection.

- Apache HTTP Server 2.4.37 with better security and performance.
- GCC Version 8.2
- The LUKS version 2 (LUKS2) format replaces the legacy LUKS (LUKS1) format for encrypting volumes
- Nginx 1.14 is available in core repository
- Varnish Cache

## Chapter 3

Minimum system requirement

Following are minimum requirement to install RHEL. However, it is ideal to have more resources than this for optimum performance of your machine

Processor	1GHz or faster
System memory (RAM)	2GB
Hard disk	20GB

Graphical installation of RHEL requires a minimum screen resolution of 800x600. If you have device with lower resolution you should do VNC installation.

Chapter 4.

Installation

In this chapter we will covers installation of Redhat Enterprise Linux version 8. The installation of RHEL is very easy and straightforward. This chapter is designed in such way even if you do not have prior knowledge of Linux you can install RHEL easily as whole installation is explained step by step with screenshots.

The summary of steps involved in installation RHEL are following:

1. **Download Media Image**

    You can download installation image from customer portal of Red hat   https://access.redhat.com/downloads , using your username and password. If you don't have username and password, Red hat allows you to have evaluation version. For Centos download the image from centos site

2. **Verify image**

    Once you finish downloading of installation image, it is good practice to verify the integrity of the downloaded image.

3. **Write image to media**

    Now write the image to required media. As this image will not fit in DVD you require Double layer DVD or you can use USB Drive.

4. **Select way, how you want install it. There are two common ways to install:-**

    1. **Interactive**

Interactive method is normal installation method, which can be either Text based or GUI. This method of installation requires user interaction for inputs during installation.

2. **Automated using Kickstart**

   For Kickstart installation, we have to create a single file containing answers to all the questions RHEL installation normally asks during interactive installation. Once the installation starts, no user intervention is required.

5. **Verify the installation**.

Interactive installation

In this section we will go through normal interactive installation of Redhat if you are installing Centos the steps are same: - .

Download Media Image

First thing first, for installation we require media. For media preparation, you have to download the installation ISO image. Open the internet explorer on your MS windows machine. Open the site of Redhat customer portal or https://access.redhat.com/downloads.

Select Red Hat Enterprise Linux 8 from the list and provide your credentials. If you do not have redhat account you can request evaluation copy. After successful login you will get list of downloads select Red Hat Enterprise Linux 8.0 Binary DVD and press Download Now

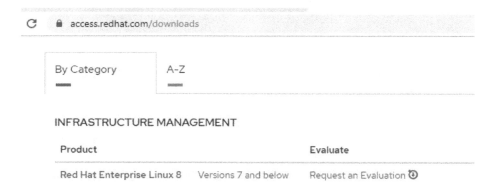

Once file has been downloaded, check the integrity of file. If you have downloaded file on MS Windows 10 computer, go to the folder in which you had downloaded the file. Press shift key and press left button of mouse.

It will open menu, press **Open PowerShell window here**

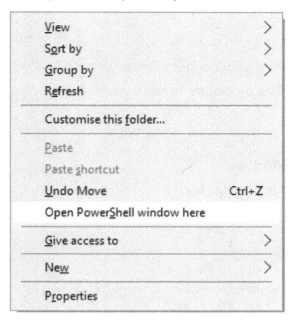

On the shell prompt give command

```
Get-FileHash -Path .\rhel-8.0-x86_64-dvd.iso -Algorithm SHA256
```

```
PS D:\Downloads> Get-FileHash -Path .\rhel-8.0-x86_64-dvd.iso -Algorithm SHA256

Algorithm       Hash
---------       ----
SHA256          005D4F88FFF6D63B0FC01A10822380EF52570EDD8834321DE7BE63002CC6CC43
```

It will show hash value, match this value with value given on the download page of the

Red Hat Enterprise Linux 8.0 Binary DVD

Last modified: 2019-04-11   SHA-256 Checksum: 005d4f88fff6d63b0fc01a10822380ef52570edd8834321de7be63002cc6cc43

Write image to media

After verification of image, you can write the ISO file to DVD. If DVD Drive in your computer is not working or not present you can write this image to USB flash drive. The procedure to write image to USB flash drive is given bellow:-

Creating USB Media on Windows

1. Download Fedora media writer from
   https://github.com/MartinBriza/MediaWriter/releases

2. Double click the downloaded file to install it and follow the Wizard.
3. Once installation is finished run **Fedora Media Writer** from start menu.
4. In the main window click Custom image and select the downloaded RedHat enterprise Linux ISO Image .
5. From the drop down menu select the drive you want to use
6. Click Write to disk . This will start the media creation process.

7. Once the process finishes and complete message appears, umount the USB device.
8. Now USB flash is ready for installation.

Steps to do installation

Booting with Media

Once media is ready. Make media as first boot device in the BOIS of computer. Check the manual of your computer to change boot priority. Once system boots, it will show Installation menu.

Select **Install RHEL Linux 8.0.0**

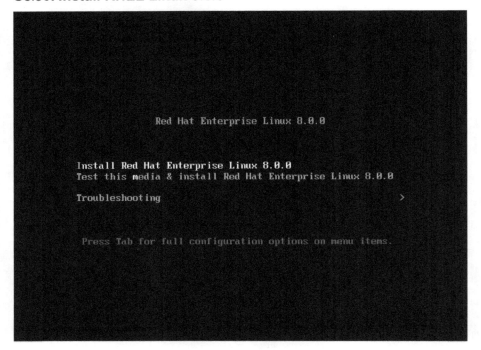

On the language menu Select the Language and press Continue

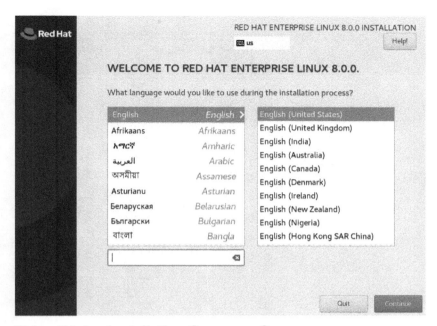

This will bring **Installation Summary** Screen.

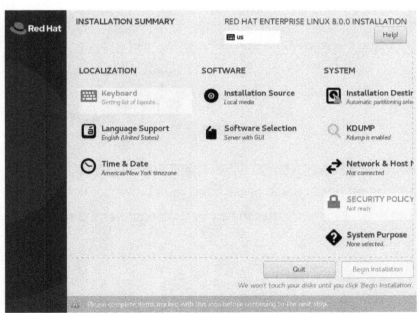

Select **Date and time** to modify date time and time zone

If you are using Network Time server for time synchronization you can

configure it here. To use network time, change the position of **Network time** button to **on** position and press small gear button for network time server settings. Once you enter the server settings press **Done**.

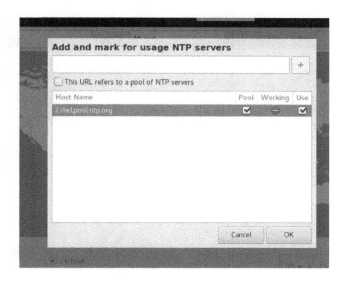

Click **Software Selection** from **Installation summary** screen and select required **Base environment**. For demo purpose I have selected **Server with GUI** and press **Done**.

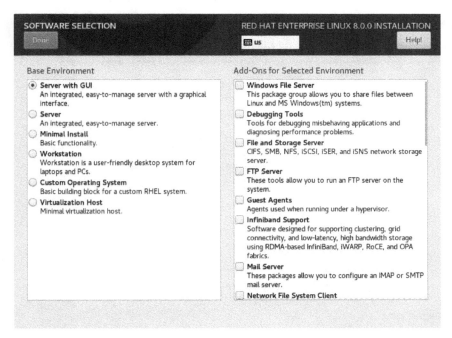

17

On Installation Summary screen, select **Installation Destination**.

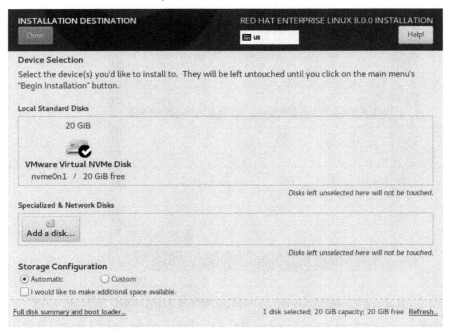

Either leave it to **Automatic Configure partitioning** or you can select **I will configure partitioning** for manual partitioning.

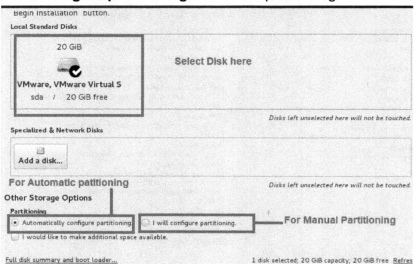

In case you select Manual partitioning, Although RedHat can works fine with two partitions root and swap but it is ideal to have minimum three partitions. These three partitions are **boot**, / (root) and **swap**. Boot should be at least 1 GB, root should at least 20GB and swap partition should be equal to or more than physical RAM in the system. You write the capacity in human readable format like 10G for 10GB and 500M for 500MB.

Now Click **Network and Host Name** for configuring network settings and hostname.

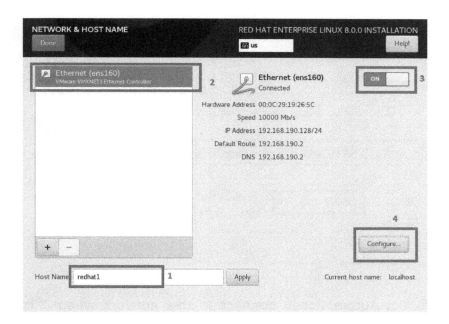

1. In **Host Name** textbox write the hostname.
2. Select the network card
3. Change Connected button to On position

4. Press configure button.

It will bring network configuration screen.

1. Select IPv4 setting tab
2. Select method as manual from drop down menu if you have static IP address otherwise leave it Automatic.
3. In case of static IP address, press Add button
4. Write down IP address, Netmask and gateway
5. Add DNS server IP Address, if you have more than one DNS server you add the IP Address separated with coma.
6. Select General Tab

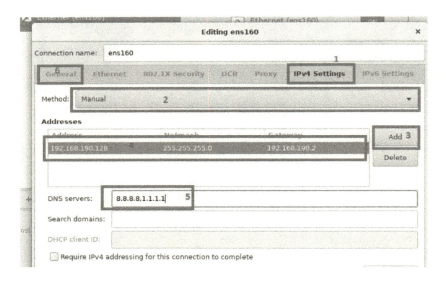

7. Select **Automatically connect to this network when it is available.** Otherwise after next boot network will not be connected automatically. Press **Save** to save setting

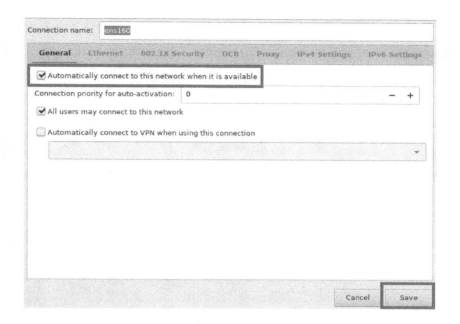

8.   Press **Done.**

Press **Begin installation**. It will bring screen on which it will show progress of installation, option to set root password and create one new users.

Select **Root password** and provide root password. Press Done.

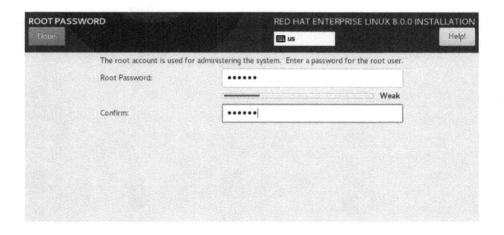

During installation, you have to create one normal user. Click **Create New** user. Provide Full name of the user, username and password and press done. If you do not want to use root user for administration you can make this user as administration by selecting **Make this user administrator**

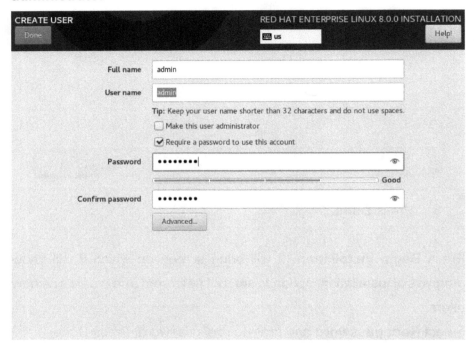

Once installation gets complete press **Reboot**.

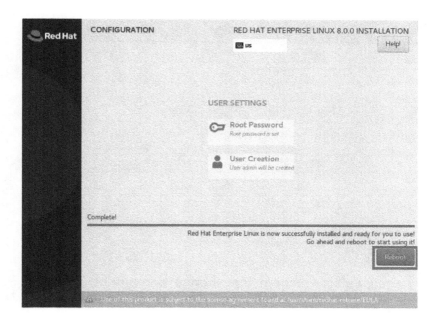

After restart system will bring screen for license and add the RedHat subscription details.

Select License information

23

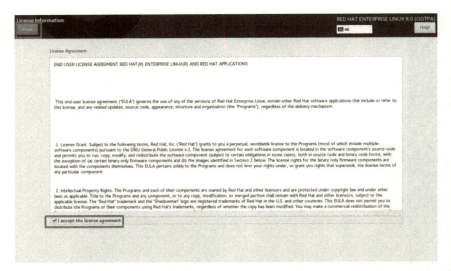

On next screen Select **I accept the license agreement** and press Done

Now press Subscription Manager (this is step is optional you can do this later on also)

On the next screen if you are using proxy provide proxy setting for connecting internet. Press **Done**.

On the next screen provide login and password for your redhat subscription and press **Done**.

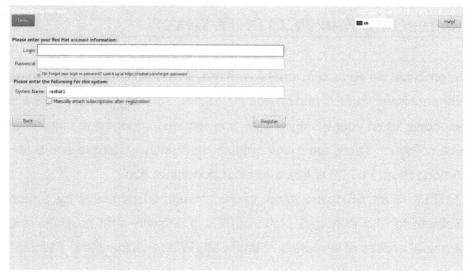

Now press **Finish Installation**.

Now you have finished your installation. It's time to connect to the newly created server from remote machine, we will discuss how to connect your windows machine in the next chapter.

Chapter 5.

Connecting Your PC to RHEL Server

In practical life you occasionally work physically on server, usually you connect from your PC and do administration. You may be using MS MS windows 10 on your PC. First thing you require to connect to Linux host is a software. There are many options like VanDyke, bitvise and putty. Among them PuTTY is free and most popular option.

PuTTY is an SSH and telnet client, developed originally by Simon Tatham for the Windows platform. It is a software that provides text terminal access of servers on remote MS Windows machine. To install putty open internet explorer and download putty from

http://www.chiark.greenend.org.uk/~sgtatham/putty/latest.html

Once you have downloaded the putty, install it.

When you run putty you will see following screen. On this screen

1. Write the IP Address of the newly installed server.

2. Select the Protocol as **SSH**

3. Give name of Session like RHEL1 or linux1 etc

4. Press **Save** button

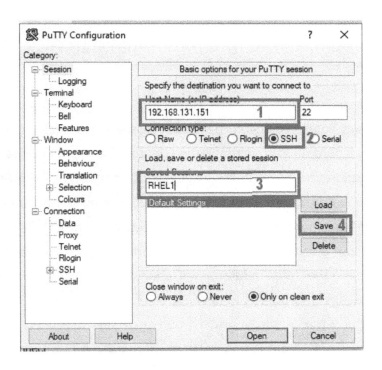

Once session is saved either double click the session name to connect to the Linux host or select the session press **Load** then press **Open**

## Chapter 6

Network

Network is group of two or more computers connected together. Network allows interconnection between different machines. You require network card on each computer to connect. Every network card has physical address known as **M**edia **A**ccess **C**ontrol address (MAC address). MAC address works on layer 2 of OSI model. Manufacturer of network interface card assigns MAC addresses to network cards. As network card can go faulty and needs replacement, with replacement of network card, the MAC address will change. To overcome this problem, we assign IP address to network card, which works on layer 3 of OSI model. As IP address are still numeric value it is difficult to remember, more over there is possibility of IP address may change in case of dynamic IPs. To make life easy for humans we use **hostname,** which nothing but name of computers.

Just to give an idea about OSI model and list of applications and devices with their respective layers, a chart is given bellow.

Seven layer of OSI and TCP Mapping

OSI Model	TCP Model	Application	Address	Devices
7:Application layer	Application Layer	HTTP / Telnet / SSH	Applications DNS, DHCP.ntp,HTTP,	
6:Presentation layer		SSL / MIME		
5: Session layer		Sockets and Remote Procedure Call (RPC)		
4: Transport layer	Transport layer	Transmission Control Protocol (TCP)	TCP/UDP	Gateway
3: Network layer	Internet layer	Internet Protocol (IP)	IP4, IP6, IPX, ICMP	Router, firewall Layer 3 switch
2: Data link layer	Network Access Layer	Ethernet / Frame Relay	MAC address, ARP	Bridge Layer 2 switch
1: Physical layer		IEEE 802.x	Ethernet	HUB

Commands to check network configuration

After fresh installation, it is good idea to check the network configuration. As a best practice note down this configuration

Show IP address

```
# ip addr show
```

Or

```
# ifconfig -a
```

Show Link status

```
# ip link show
```

Show routing table

```
# ip route
```

Or

```
# netstat -rn
```

Check and change hostname

Show hostname

```
# hostname
```

Change hostname

Whenever you want to change hostname, you have to change it in two steps

1. Change hostname using command **hostnamectl**
2. Next change entry in /etc/hosts

1. Give hostnamectl command status to check the current

```
# hostnamectl status
   Static hostname: RHEL1
         Icon name: computer
           Chassis: n/a
        Machine ID: 98c0429d893c48b88fba101f95aa70ca
           Boot ID: 864f0f4e99cd4442b4f388a15a7fc132
```

Or

```
# hostname
```

2. Change the hostname

```
# hostnamectl set-hostname RHEL2
```

3. Next step is to change **/etc/hosts** file

```
127.0.0.1 RHEL2 localhost.localdomain localhost
```

Setting Up the DNS Name Resolution

Whenever you write hostname instead of IP address to ping or to connect Linux host. You have multiple option to resolve hostname to IP address.

- Local file i.e. /etc/hosts
- DNS server
- NIS

Local file (/etc/hosts)

/etc/hosts is file which stores hostname to IP address mapping. It provides ability to resolve hostname without using DNS server. We generally use this file if we are connecting to limited number of host due scope or security reason. But problem in using this file is that if host changes its ipaddress for any reason then administrator has to change this file on all servers or PC who wants to resolve this hostname.

Format

IP_address   hostname aliases

Example

```
127.0.0.1                RHEL1 localhost
```

```
::1                           RHEL1 localhost
192.168.228.129               RHEL1
```

DNS

A DNS server is a central repository that contains a database of public IP addresses and their associated hostnames. Whenever any client wants to resolve hostname to IP address instead of using its local file it sends request to DNS server. If IP Address of some client changes you just have to update the DNS entry. You can have multiple DNS server in one organization. To redirect your request for hostname resolution RedHat uses resolve.conf file which is present. in /etc directory

/etc/resolv.conf

/etc/resolv.conf is required in case DNS is used to resolve host names. You need to put your DNS server IP addresses in this file. Generally, you need one name server, but you can include up to three if you want redundancy. If the first one on the list is not responding, system tries to resolve against the next one on the list, and so on.

Edit **/etc/resolv.conf** to add list of name servers, like this:

```
nameserver 8.8.8.8
nameserver 8.8.8.9
nameserver 1.2.3.6
```

NIS

Network Information Service (NIS) was developed by Sun Microsystems as a way to share information among all computers in a local area network. Of many tasks NIS can also be used for Name resolution.

Changing order for hostname resolution

/etc/nsswitch.conf

If hosts file and DNS configuration is there in **resolv.conf** in your server, Whenever you do hostname resolution the system looks for local file **(/etc/hosts)** for entry of hostname and respective IP address. If there is no entry, it looks for **/etc/resolv.conf** file for DNS configuration. If there is no DNS configuration also then it will check for NIS configuration. However, you can change this behavior by changing order in **/etc/nsswitch.conf** file.

```
vi /etc/nsswitch.conf
```

```
#hosts:        db files nisplus nis dns
hosts:         files dns
```

In this example search sequence is first files means **/etc/hosts** then DNS server.

Network Manager

NetworkManager is daemon which provides interface for easy configuration and management of Network Connectivity.   In the previous versions of RHEL, Network configuration was handled using files. However, in RedHat 8 it is handled by network manager. Network manager is a dynamic network configuration and control daemon. It can manage network interface like Wifi , Ethernet and mobile devices. Network manager can switch network automatically from wired to WiFi incase wired network is unavailable and vice versa.

If you are coming from older version of RedHat and use to use network scrirts like ifup and ifdown, In RedHat 8 ifup and ifdown scripts has been deprecated, now it is handled by network manager. The ifcfg configuration files which were used traditionally, still supported in RHEL but not available by default.

Network Manager configures
1. IP address
2. Static routes
3. Network aliases
4. VPN configuration
5. DNS information

Check the status of networkmanager daemon

```
# systemctl status NetworkManager
```

Start Networkmanager if it is not working

```
# systemctl start NetworkManager
```

Enable it to start automatically with system start (Most of the time it is not required as networkmanager is configured to start automatically by default)

```
# systemctl enable NetworkManager
```

Set up Static IP Address using Graphical interface

To set static IP address following steps are there
6. Login as root
7. Click network manager icon and select Wired settings

8. Click setting icon, small 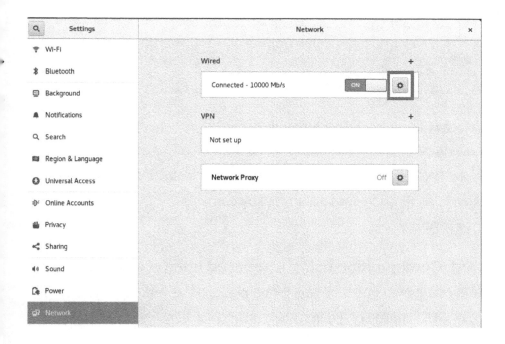 gear

9. Select IPv4 tab settings

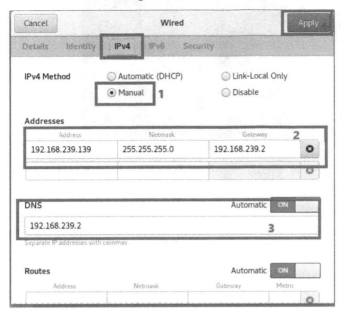

1. Select **Manual** from IPv4 Method.
2. Provide IP address, Netmask and Gateway.
3. Write DNS server IP address. If you have more than one DNS provide all IP addresses separated by commas.
4. Press **Apply.**

Network Configuration using text based interface nmtui

Nmtui is text based interface tool for configuring networking. If you do not have GUI installed on your system, this tool is very helpful specially if you are administrating system remotely. This tool is installed by default with RHEL server installation. In case it is not there you can install it.

```
# yum install NetworkManager-tui
```

To start nmtui

```
# nmtui
```

Commands

Edit the connection setting

Syntax

```
nmtui edit connection_name
```

Example

```
# nmtui edit ens33
```

Connect the disconnected connection

Syntax

```
nmtui connect connection_name
```

Example

```
# nmtui connect ens33
```

Change hostname using nmtui

Syntax

```
nmtui hostname new_hostname
```

Example

```
# nmtui hostname RHEL2
```

Navigate NMTUI

As nmtui is a text based user interface you have to use keyboard for navigation. To move the cursor to next field press TAB key, use SHIFT + TAB to move backward . Use SPACE bar key for drop down menu.

Modifying IP address using NMTUI

Start nmtui

```
# nmtui
```

1. Select **Edit a connection**

2. Select the connection profile from the list and press **Edit**

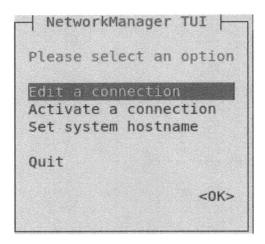

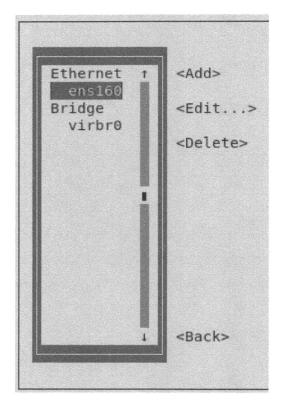

3. From the next screen press SPACEBAR key on the IPv4 configuration to get popup menu.

   1. Select **Manual** to set static IP address.

   2. Press TAB key to move to Address field and provide IP Address with Netmask .

   3. Press TAB key to move to Gateway column and provide Gateway.

   4. Press TAB for DNS Servers. Press SPACE key to add DNS server. You can add more than one DNS server.

   5. Make sure Automatically connect is selected.

   6. Press OK

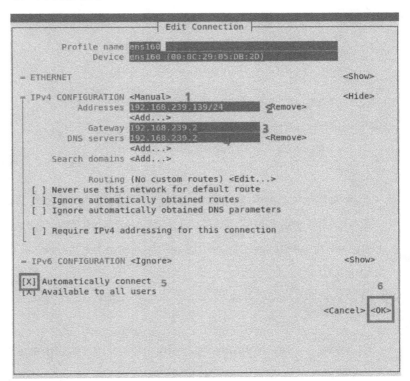

7. Press ESC key to come out from NMTUI

Modifying network configuration using configuration files

If you are old school guy like me, who enjoy in working with configuration files instead of GUI. Although in RHEL8 configuration files has been deprecated you can still use configuration files to control networking. In this example, I will explain how to change IP address of host using configuration files.

Changing IP address using configuration files

1. Check current setting

```
# ip addr show
```

2. Check current devices

```
[root@RHEL2]# nmcli d
DEVICE   TYPE      STATE       CONNECTION
ens33    ethernet  connected   ens160
lo       loopback  unmanaged   --
```

3. Edit **/etc/sysconfig/network-scripts/ifcfg-***. Where **ifcfg-*** file is device file you just checked in last command. The command output shows **ens160** as device name then the file name will be **ifcfg-ens160**

```
# vi /etc/sysconfig/network-scripts/ifcfg-ens160
```

4. Change **/etc/sysconfig/network-scripts/ifcfg-ens160** file depending on whether you have static IP address or you are using DHCP

40

Static	DHCP
DEVICE=ens160	DEVICE=ens160
BOOTPROTO=static	BOOTPROTO=dhcp
IPADDR =192.168.0.132	
NETMASK=255.255.255.0	
GATEWAY=192.168.0.1	
ONBOOT=yes	

5. Restart network connection to change IP address without rebooting. For that we will switch off and on the network connection. Unlike the previous version of RedHat where you use to restart the network services, in the current version it recommended the NetworkManager.service daemon should always running. Instead you use nmcli command to bring connection down and up. Moreover ifup and ifdown scripts has also been deprecated. If you use these ifup and ifdown scripts in new version, it calls nmcli command.

```
# nmcli con down ens160
# nmcli con up ens160
```

Network Scripts

As mentioned the support for network scripts is deprecated in Red Hat Enterprise Linux 8. In RHEL 8 even the ifup and ifdown scripts has been replaced with newer version which call the NetworkManager service through the nmcli tool. By Default, that custom commands in /sbin/ifup-local, ifdown-pre-local and ifdown-local scripts are not executed.

If you really require any of these scripts, you can still install deprecated network scripts in the system with the following command:

```
# yum install network-scripts
```

Changing DNS server using configuration file

Edit /etc/resolv.conf and add the ebtries for DNS server

```
search example.com        // give own FQDN
nameserver 8.8.8.8        // IPaddress of first DNS
nameserver 8.8.4.4        // IPaddress of Second DNS
```

NMCLI

NetworkManager Command Line Interface is command line utility for for controlling NetworkManager. It is also used for reporting status of network. The main use of this utility is in Servers, Headless machines, terminals and by power users who prefer to use command line. NMCLI is ideal tool used in scripts . Few examples of the nmcli are given bellow :-

Display the overall status of NetworkManager.

```
# nmcli general status
```

Display all connections

```
# nmcli connection show -a
```

Display only active connections

```
# nmcli connection show -active
```

Display a list of devices recognized by NetworkManager and their current state.

```
# nmcli device status
```

Bring down Ethernet interface

Syntax

```
nmcli connection down interface_name
```

Example

```
# nmcli connection down ens160
```

Bring up Ethernet interface

Syntax

```
nmcli connection up interface_name
```

Example

```
# nmcli connection up ens160
```

Change IP address using nmcli

Syntax

```
nmcli connection modify interface_name IPv4.address <ipaddr>/netmask
```

Example

```
# nmcli connection modify ens160 IPv4.address 192.168.239.141/24
```

Important Network Commands

Task	Command

Check connectivity between two systems	`ping IP_address of other system`
	`Example`
	`ping 10.1.1.2`

Check IP address configuration	`ifconfig -a`
	`or`
	`ip addr show`

Check configuration of network card	`cat /etc/sysconfig/network-scripts/ifcfg-*`
Check routing table	`ip route show`
Querying DNS	`dig`
Local file to resolve hosts to IP address	`/etc/hosts`
DNS server configuration file	`/etc/resolv.conf`

## Chapter 7

Users Management

User management describes the ability of administrators to manage user access to resources of the server and attached devices. In multiuser environment it is recommended for security and privacy purpose to create separate username for each user so that every user can keep his data in their respective home folder. The control of users and groups is a central part of system administration.

User and group

A **user** is anyone who uses a computer or network service. A user can be ether human or an accounts. For better management, the users are grouped together in **groups**. Group is logical entity to organize users together based on their different properties, it can be either based on same department, same place or same work. Sometimes groups are just made to provide certain common facilities or right to different users.

Root user V/S normal user

At the time of installation, the installation screen gives option to create the password for root user and additional one user. You can also assign this additional user with root privileges on same screen. In RHEL Linux root is the default administrator of the system. Root is the most powerful user among all users on RHEL server. Once you login as a root user, you can do anything on the server. Unlike normal user, root user can read write and modify the files and directories of all other users. **root** user can even modify and delete system files also. Hence, it is absolutely important to keep the root user's password in safe custody.

Login as root user on graphical terminal

If Graphical desktop environment is installed, after system boot you will get the login screen.

Press the user's icon to login as normal user

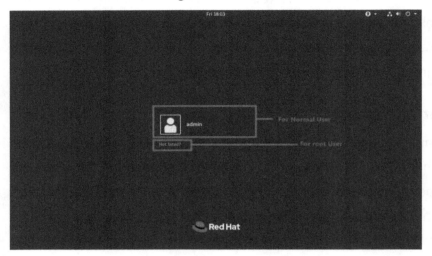

To login as root user, you select **Not listed?** from the graphical login screen.

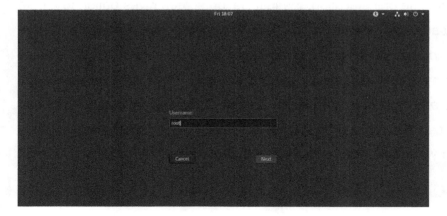

Once text box for login name appears type **root** and press **ENTER**, type the root's password that you selected during installation at the password prompt, and press **ENTER**.

User Management using GUI

To create user in RHEL.

1. Login as root user.

2. Click **Activities** from panel and write users in search bar, click **users**. It will open **users** administration windows .

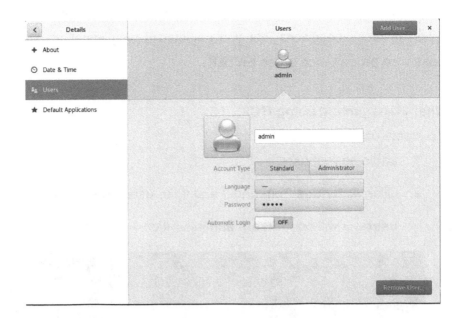

3. To add user press Add User button. It will bring another dialog box with following fields

Account Type: You have two options Standard or administrator

Full Name : Type Full name of the user

Username : Type username of user you want to create
Allow User to set password when they next login/Set a password now : There are two ways to set password. First way, you can force user to set password on next login. Other way is by setting temporary password by administrator so that new user can change password at his convenience. This way you add additional security layer so that no unauthorized user can use newly created username before user sets password.

Users management using Command Line

User management using command line is very interesting and it offers more options and flexibility.

Add User

Syntax

```
# useradd -c "Full name of user" username
```

Example

```
# useradd -c "Adam mark" adam1
```

Now set the password

Syntax

```
# passwd username
```

Example

```
# passwd  adam1
```

Modify user

Syntax

```
# usermod option username
```

Example

```
# usermod -c "Adam markwell" adam1
```

Delete/remove user

Syntax

```
# userdel username
```

Example

```
# userdel adam1
```

Display information about user

Show current user's information

Syntax

```
$ id
```

Example

```
$ id
```

Show information of other users

50

Syntax

```
# id username
```

Example

```
# id admin
```

Change password for other user

Syntax

```
# passwd username
```

Example

```
# passwd admin
```

Change own password

```
$ passwd
```

List password expiry information

Synatx

```
# chage -l username
```

Example

```
# chage -l admin
```

Set password expiry

root user can set the password expiry date for any user. In this example password will expire after 10 from last password change.

Syntax

```
# chage -M no of days from last password change username
```

Example

```
# chage -l admin
```

```
[root@redhat1 ~]# chage -l admin
Last password change                                  : never
Password expires                                      : never
Password inactive                                     : never
Account expires                                       : never
Minimum number of days between password change        : 0
Maximum number of days between password change        : 99999
Number of days of warning before password expires     : 7
[root@redhat1 ~]#
```

```
# chage -M 10  adam1
```

```
# chage -l adam1
```

```
[root@redhat1 ~]# chage -l admin
Last password change                                  : never
Password expires                                      : never
Password inactive                                     : never
Account expires                                       : never
Minimum number of days between password change        : 0
Maximum number of days between password change        : 10
Number of days of warning before password expires     : 7
[root@redhat1 ~]#
```

Disable password expiration for user

Syntax

```
# chage –M 99999 username
```

Example

```
# chage -M 99999 admin
```

```
[root@redhat1 ~]# chage -M 99999 admin
[root@redhat1 ~]# chage -l admin
Last password change                                  : never
Password expires                                      : never
Password inactive                                     : never
Account expires                                       : never
Minimum number of days between password change        : 0
Maximum number of days between password change        : 99999
Number of days of warning before password expires     : 7
[root@redhat1 ~]#
```

Force user to change password at next login
Syntax
```
# chage -d0 username
```
Example
```
# chage -d0 adam1
```

Lock user
Syntax
```
# usermod -L username
```
Example
```
# usermod -L adam1
```

Unlock user
Syntax
```
# usermod -U username
```
Example
```
# usermod -U adam1
```

UID

Unique User ID better known as UID. For every user that exist on system has UID. UID is numerical representation of every user. For root user it is 0. For regular users it starts from 1000.

User	UID
root	0
System user	1 – 999
Regular users	1000 +

Groups

Every user we create belongs at least one group and all groups have their group ID. **/etc/group** file contains list of all available groups and their member users.

There are two type of groups:-

- Primary group
- Secondary group

Primary group

When you create a new user a new group of same name also gets created and the new user become member of that group. This is the group applied to your login and used by default when you create new files and directories. Primary group ID is written in **/etc/passwd** file for respective users in the third field.

Secondary Group

These are the groups users are member other than primary group.

Changing secondary group

```
# usermod –G data2 user1
Where user1 is user and data2 is group and G option for
assigning secondary group
```

Add new group

Syntax

```
# groupadd groupname
```

Example

```
# groupadd data1
```

Delete group

Syntax

```
# groupdel groupname
```

Example

```
# groupdel data1
```

/etc/group file

/etc/group files stores the group information. There is one entry per line for each group and each line has the fields separated by a colon (:) .

```
groupname:password:GID:grouplist
```

Field	Description
Groupname	Name of group.
password	This is useful to implement privileged groups. Generally, password is not used. It can store encrypted password.
GID	Group ID
Group List	List of all users who are members of the group. Commas must separate the user names.

Example

```
science:x:1003:class1, class2
```

/etc/passwd

passwd file in the /etc directory stores information of all users. The information in /etc/passwd file is required during login. It is a plain text file, which contains list of the system's accounts. Like /etc/group file there is one entry per line for each user, and each line has the fields separated by a colon (:) containing information like user ID, group ID, home directory, shell, etc. Only root user has write permission for this file.

Format

```
username:x:UID:GID:Full_user_name:home_directory:shell
```

```
sshd:x:74:74:Privilege-separated SSH:/var/empty/sshd:/sbin/nologin
insights:x:978:976:Red Hat Insights:/var/lib/insights:/sbin/nologin
avahi:x:70:70:Avahi mDNS/DNS-SD Stack:/var/run/avahi-daemon:/sbin/nologin
tcpdump:x:72:72::/:/sbin/nologin
admin:x:1000:1000:admin:/home/admin:/bin/bash
[root@redhat1 ~]#
```

Field	Description
Username	Username of the user. It should be unique and can be up to 8 characters. It is also case-sensitive
x	An x character indicates that encrypted password is stored in **/etc/shadow** file.
UID	User ID
GID	Group ID
Full_user_name	Full name of the user
Home directory	Home directory of the user is specified here where user will keep his files.
shell	Default shell for user, normally set to "/bin/bash" but it can be /etc/ksh , /etc/csh or any other shell

Example

```
adam1:x:1004:1004:Adam mark:/home/adam1:/bin/bash
```

/etc/shadow

Stores actual password in encrypted format

Format

```
username:password:last_password_change:minimum
```

Field	Description
Username	Up to 8 characters. Case-sensitive, usually all lowercase. A direct match to the username in the /etc/passwd file.
Password	13 character encrypted password. A blank entry indicates a password is not required to log in (usually a bad idea), and a " * " indicates account has been disabled.
Last_password_change	Date of last password change. Expressed in numbers of days since January 1, 1970
Minimum	The number of days before password may be changed (0 indicates it may be changed at any time)
Maximum	The number of days after which password must be changed (99999 indicates user can keep his or her password unchanged for many, many years)
Warn	Number of days to warn user of an expiring password (7 for a full week)

Inactive	The number of days after password expires that account is disabled
Expire	Date of expiration expressed in number of days since January 1, 1970. (After that Account will disabled)

Example

```
avahi:!!:18154::::::
tcpdump:!!:18154::::::
admin:$6$kTFg1ikXMH8KkUbx$mHW33yGf6FLSarZ1I0YHE27cSjlvkJPqac1tD398QmhZ0RfAB42nMEMQWcIbfPhpzpGnIGKanLT8uG7LGkiR2.::0:99999:7:
[root@redhat1 ~]#
```

```
user1:$6$0UseZ0gR$yxl3B9SilhVjpu6epAlir1:17261:0:99999:7:::
```

Chapter 8.

Software management

Every Linux distribution has set of packages that gets installed with installation. As an organization, you may require some more software according to your requirement, like you may be using this server as web server so you require Apache or other http server. For additional software installation, you require packages. Package is a bundle of all executables and data files in to single file. There are two types of packages are available

1. **Source code packages**
    Bundle of files related to one program, which includes source code, configuration files and documentation.
2. **Binary Packages**
    Binary package is bundle of precompiled binary files and its metadata files.

Package distribution formats

As mentioned packages are of two types, hence distributed in either binary or source code format. The main package distribution systems are :-

Redhat Package Manager

As name suggests this format was introduced by Redhat. This format is not only used by Redhat based distribution like RHEL and Fedora but also adopted by many other distributions like SUSE and Mandriva. RPM packages uses files with .rpm extension.

DEBian package manager

This package distribution system was introduced by Debian. Mainly used by Debian and Debian based distributions like Ubuntu, Linux Mint and PureOS. It uses files with .deb extension.

Source Code Packages

Source code packages can be distributed in to two formats

1. **Tarball files**

    Tarball package distribution is conventional type of package distribution. These type of packages are available from any third-party software providers and require **make** utility to compile.

2. **SRPM**

    Redhat based distributions provide repositories from where you can download source code of available binaries we call these files as SRPMS or source RPMs. SRPMs are rpm packages containing only the source code, rpm spec files which can be installed with rpm and then can be compiled or modified manually.

Package metadata

RHEL uses .rpm packages for installing software with rpm command. RPM package is simply a file that contains some files and information about those files. Technically speaking RPM is a file containing **cpio** archive and metadata about itself. RPM Header contains the metadata and this metadata is used to determine following things about the package:-

- Description of package.

- List of files in the package.

- Version and release of package.

- When and who made it.

- Architecture supported.

- Checksums of the files contained in the package.

- Dependences.

  Etc…

Package Management System

If you try to install single package manually you have to first install all its dependences and keep track of versions also. To make software management easy Linux companies had developed a system known as package management system or package manager. Package management system install precompiled packages, which are archives that contains binaries of software, configuration files, and information about dependencies. Package management system is a collection of software tools to automate the process of installation, upgradation and removal of software packages. Software manager maintains its own database of software dependencies and version information. Package management system helps in preventing software mismatches and missing prerequisites. RHEL uses YUM tool for package management.

YUM

Like other Linux distributions, RHEL has very comprehensive package management system known as **YUM. Y**ellow dog **U**pdater **M**odifier is command line tool for package management. Yum uses repositories to fetch the correct version of a particular package compatible for your system. Yum allows automatic updating of packages and dependency management. When you use yum command for installation of software, it automatically downloads package and all its dependencies from the defined repositories. In RHEL version 8 uses YUM v4 instead to YUM v3 used on RHEL 7. YUM v4 tool, which is based on the DNF technology has the following advantages over the previous YUM v3 used on RHEL 7:

- Better performance
- Support for modular content (We will discuss later about modules)
- Stable API for integration with tooling

Modules

IN RHEL 8 new concept of modules has been introduced. Modules is the extension to RPM. A module is set of RPM packages that represent a component. A module typically contains application packages, its libraries, dependent packages and documentation including help files for these packages. Now in RHEL 8 can contain multiple versions of same package for example you can have two versions of python or perl. These packages have its own life cycle rather than RHEL life cycle. When you install one version of module its dependences and libraries will be automatically installed from the module. You can consider module as virtual repository. For handling module `yum module` command has been introduced. The modules has extension module after rpm like abc.rpm.module.

Repository

Yum repository is collection of RPM packages with metadata that is used by Yum Command. It is way of distributing content in any Linux

63

Distribution. It can be present locally (DVD, directory) or remotely (FTP, HTTP, HTTPS). The package manager uses repositories to install, remove, and upgrade packages. The configuration file for yum repositories is **/etc/yum.conf**. To define repositories you can use this file. However, it is recommended to create or use existing **.repo** file in the **/etc/yum.repos.d/** directory for defining repositories. Redhat 8 is now distributed through two main repositories.

- BaseOS
- Appstream

There is no extras channel in RHEL 8. BaseOS and AppStream contains all software packages, which were available in extras and optional repositories in earlier version of RHEL.

BaseOS

BaseOS is intended to provide core set of functionality and core component to OS independent all type of installation. Which mean BaseOS repository is required for all set of installation even for headless installation.

Appstream

Appstream contains additional userspace applications, languages, databases etc. Appstream is intended for different set of workloads. For example if you want make this server as http server or want install database. Appstream is updated more frequently than BaseOS. Appstream is made up of rpm packages and modules.

If you think required software is not available in the RedHat repositories, you have option to add third party repositories like rpmfusion, epel etc. You can easily install various packages by using these third party repositories. Please note that these packages are not officially supported by Red Hat, Inc, but provides many popular packages and apps. For example epel repository is required to install openvpn server.

RedHat Subscription

Unlike license fee models Redhat implements subscription model. In the subscription you don't pay any upfront fee, you just pay fees for yearly subscription per machine. This subscription model offers different type of support to the customer depending upon the type of subscription. Best part of this model is that you do not have to pay for any upgradation fee if new version comes and your subscription is active you can freely download and use that version. You will get same support what you were getting with older version. Broadly three types of subscriptions are there

- Self support
- Standard
- Premium

Self support

Offers only download and updates

Standard support

Offers support via web and phone

Premium support

Offers support via web and phone but additionally the response time is much quicker than standard support. For example, for severity 1 problem response time is 1 business hour in case of standard support and for premium it is one hour. The difference is that business hours can be 9 to 5 depending on the region and there will be no support after that, so if you have any problem in the Redhat you have to wait for next business day. Moreover, there is no support on holidays if support is only for business hours.

Registering system with RedHat subscription

There are two ways to register your server with Redhat

1. At the time of initial configuration after installation
2. Using subscription-manager command any time after installation.

The command to register for subscription

```
# subscription-manager register --username username --password password --auto-attach
```

```
[root@redhat1 ~]# subscription-manager register --username ▓▓▓▓ --password ▓▓▓▓▓ --auto-attach
Registering to: subscription.rhsm.redhat.com:443/subscription
The system has been registered with ID: 6▓10188-81▓▓-4873-8f6d-1▓▓▓▓▓
The registered system name is: redhat1
Installed Product Current Status:
Product Name: Red Hat Enterprise Linux for x86_64
Status:        Subscribed
```

To check the subscription

```
#subscription-manager list
```

Or

```
#subscription manager list --consumed
```

Package management using Yum

List all installed and available software

```
# yum list
```

List all available software

```
# yum list available
```

List all installed software

```
# yum list installed
```

Search the package name with keyword

Syntax

```
# yum search keyword
```

Example

```
# yum search bzip2
```

Display information about the package

Syntax

```
# yum info package_name
```

Example

```
# yum info zip
```

Install package

Syntax

```
# yum install -y package_name
```

Example

```
# yum install -y firefox
```

Remove package

Syntax

```
# yum remove package_name
```

67

Example

```
# yum remove firefox
```

Check which package provides specific file

Syntax

```
# yum provides file-name
```

Example

```
# yum provides /etc/hosts
```

Get help

```
# yum help
```

Check for Available Updates

```
# yum check-update
```

Update all software provided by enabled repositories

```
# yum update
```

Clean the yum cache

```
# yum clean all
```

Interactive shell

```
# yum shell
```

List yum history

```
# yum history list
```

Package group

Package group is group of software, which have same motive to install such as development tools, web server, desktop etc. It makes administrator's life easy by installing and downloading dependent software automatically. For example, you want to install backup client you will give command **yum group install "Backup Client"**

List all package group available

```
# yum group list
```

Install group package

Syntax

```
yum group install package_name
```

Example

```
# yum group install "Backup Client"
```

Remove package group

Syntax

```
yum group remove package_name
```

Example

```
# yum group remove "Backup Client"
```

Information about group package

Syntax

```
# yum group info package_name
```

Example

```
# yum group info "Development Tools"
```

Modules

Streams and profiles

Module Streams

Modules are available in one or multiple streams which usually represent a version of a software, giving you an option to choose what versions of packages you want to install. Module stream is like virtual repository. Each module may have a default stream which usually provides the latest or recommended version of the component. Default streams make it easy to install packages without the need to learn about modules. Modules make it possible to have multiple versions of software available to your system for installation.

Module Profiles

To simplify installation further, modules usually classified with set of specific set of packages for specific workload or user case. This list of packages is known as profile. A profile name can be anything like server, client, development, minimal install etc.

Package management using modules

List all available modules

```
# yum module list
```

```
[root@redhat1 /]# yum module list
Updating Subscription Management repositories.
Last metadata expiration check: 0:03:11 ago on Sat 02 Nov 2019 07:21:35 PM +04.
Red Hat Enterprise Linux 8 for x86_64 - AppStream (RPMs)
Name              Stream       Profiles            Summary
389-ds            1.4                              389 Directory Server (base)
ant               1.10 [d]     common [d]          Java build tool
container-tools   1.0          common [d]          Common tools and dependencies for container runtimes
container-tools   rhel8 [d]    common [d]          Common tools and dependencies for container runtimes
freeradius        3.0 [d]      server [d]          High-performance and highly configurable free RADIUS ser
                                                   ver
gimp              2.8 [d]      common [d], devel   gimp module
```

It will show output in four columns

- Name of the module
- Stream
- Profile
- Summary

The output shows Steams and profiles with [d], [e], [x] and [i] in the stream and profile column which show the status of module's stream and profile. Where [d] if for default, [e] for enabled [x] for disabled [i] installed.

Display information about specific module

Syntax

```
yum module info module_name
```

Example

```
# yum module info
```

Display profile information of particular module

Syntax

```
yum module info --profile module_name
```

Example

```
# yum module info –profile gimp
```

Find out which modules provide a package

Syntax

```
# yum module provides package
```

71

Example

```
# yum module provides gimp
```

Display current status of module

Syntax

```
Yum module list module_name
```

Example

```
# yum module list gimp
```

Enabling Module

Enable the module when you wish to make the packages available for installation.

Enable a module using its default stream

Syntax

```
yum module enable module-name
```

Example

```
yum module enable gimp
```

Enable a module without default stream

Modules which do not have default streams, you must explicitly specify the stream.

Syntax

yum module enable module-name:stream

Example

```
# yum module enable 389-ds:1.4
```

Installing module

Syntax

```
yum install module module_name
```

Example

```
# yum install module gimp
Or
# yum install @gimp
```

This command will install default stream and default profile of the module. This command is very useful, in case you do not care about version and workload. But default stream should be enabled

Installing non default Stream

List the available Streams

```
# yum module list perl
```

```
perl            5.24            common [d], minimal
perl            5.26 [d]        common [d], minimal
```

Install specific stream

```
# yum install @perl:5.24
```

This command will install perl 5.24 version instead of default version which 5.26

Installing non default profile of an application

```
# yum module list gimp
# yum install @gimp/devel
```

This command will install gimp software suited for development environment.

73

Installing non-default profile and non-default stream

```
# yum module install Module_name:stream/profile
```

Removing modules

In general, to remove a module installed on your system, use the following command:

Syntax

```
# yum module remove module_name:stream/profile
```

Example

```
# yum module remove gimp/devel
```

Resetting module streams

The reset command of modules returns all of its streams to their initial state which is neither enabled nor disabled. If the module has a default stream, that stream becomes active.

```
[root@redhat1 ~]# yum module reset php
Updating Subscription Management repositories.
Unable to read consumer identity
This system is not registered to Red Hat Subscription Management. You can use subscr
Last metadata expiration check: 0:23:32 ago on Wed 06 Nov 2019 07:51:49 PM +04.
Dependencies resolved.
================================================================================
 Package                       Arch                      Version
================================================================================
Resetting module streams:
 php                                                     7.2

Transaction Summary
================================================================================

Is this ok [y/N]: y
Complete!
```

Syntax

```
# yum module reset module-name
```

Example

```
# yum module reset php
```

74

Disable a module and all its streams

Syntax

```
# yum module disable module-name
```

Example

```
# yum module disable php
```

```
[root@redhat1 ~]# yum module disable  php
Updating Subscription Management repositories.
Unable to read consumer identity
This system is not registered to Red Hat Subscription Management. You can
Last metadata expiration check: 0:26:53 ago on Wed 06 Nov 2019 07:51:49 PM
Dependencies resolved.
================================================================================
 Package                        Arch                             Version
================================================================================
Disabling module streams:
 php

Transaction Summary
================================================================================

Is this ok [y/N]: y
Complete!
[root@redhat1 ~]#
```

Package management using RPM

RPM stands for **R**ed Hat **P**ackage **M**anager. RPM packages have **.rpm** extension. **rpm** command is used to manage software which include listing, installing, updating and removing rpm packages. RPM is usually used to install packages that have been downloaded locally.

Install

Syntax

```
rpm -ihv  package_name
```

Example

```
# rpm -ihv zip-3.0-11.el7.x86_64.rpm
```

Update

Syntax

```
rpm -Uhv package_name
```

Example

```
# rpm -Uhv zip-3.0-11.el7.x86_64.rpm
```

Remove

Syntax

```
rpm -ev package_name
```

Example

```
# rpm -ev zip
```

Query all installed packages

Syntax

```
rpm -qa
```

Display detailed information about package

Syntax

```
rpm -qi package_name
```

Example

```
# rpm -qi zip
```

Find the file belongs to which package

Syntax

```
rpm -qf  path_to_the_file
```

Example

```
# rpm -qf /etc/hosts
setup-2.8.71-4.el7.noarch
```

Find out all dependences

Syntax

```
rpm -qpR package_name
```

Example

```
# rpm -qpR zip-3.0-11.el7.x86_64.rpm
libbz2.so.1()(64bit)
libc.so.6()(64bit)
libc.so.6(GLIBC_2.14)(64bit)
libc.so.6(GLIBC_2.2.5)(64bit)
libc.so.6(GLIBC_2.3)(64bit)
libc.so.6(GLIBC_2.3.4)(64bit)
libc.so.6(GLIBC_2.4)(64bit)
<- Output Truncated ->
```

Repository

As mentioned repositories are collection of RPM packages with metadata that is used by Yum Command. This is a better way of distributing contents of Linux distributions. Repositories make sure you get safe and authentic contents. As most of the time we use repositories on the internet the authenticity of the content of the repository which we download is pristine requirement. Moreover, the download should also be in secured manner. The Red hat ensures it uses end to end security of the RPM packages. First thing is by using https site instead to http site which makes sure that the contents are distributed over secured channel. The Redhat uses separate Public key infrastructure. For RPM Package security RPM package signatures can be used to implement cryptographic integrity checks for RPM packages. At the time of RPM package installation these signatures can be verified as it is part of the RPM package. To enable RPM signature checking the yum repository file must contain a **gpgcheck=1** line, as in the following example:-

```
[myrepo]
name=My Repository
baseurl=https:///download.myrepoex.com/version8/
enabled=1
gpgcheck=1
```

Working with repositories

Display all enabled repositories

```
# yum repolist
```

```
[root@redhat1 /]# yum  repolist
Updating Subscription Management repositories.
Extra Packages for Enterprise Linux 8 - x86_64          2.4 kB/s | 4.6 kB      00:01
repo id                           repo name                                                status
*epel                             Extra Packages for Enterprise Linux 8 - x86_64     2,837
rhel-8-for-x86_64-appstream-rpms  Red Hat Enterprise Linux 8 for x86_64 - AppStream ( 6,050
rhel-8-for-x86_64-baseos-rpms     Red Hat Enterprise Linux 8 for x86_64 - BaseOS (RPM 2,206
[root@redhat1 /]#
```

Display all repositories enabled and disabled

```
# yum repolist all
```

Display packages for specific repository

```
# yum list |grep baseos
```

Add / Enable / Disable repositories

Using yum-config-manager command to enable/add/disable repositories. You need to install `yum-utils` to use `yum-config-manager`

78

```
# yum install yum-utils
```

Disable already enabled repository

First list all repositories

```
# yum repolist all
```

Disable the repository

To enable and disable the repository use repository id which you will get through list command

Syntax

```
# yum-config-manager --disable repository_id
```

Example

```
# yum-config-manager --disable InstallMedia-AppStream
```

```
[root@redhat1 ~]# yum repolist all
Updating Subscription Management repositories.
Unable to read consumer identity
This system is not registered to Red Hat Subscription Management. You can use subscriptio
n-manager to register.
Last metadata expiration check: 22:33:39 ago on Fri 08 Nov 2019 11:41:34 AM +04.
repo id                        repo name                              status
InstallMedia-AppStream         Red Hat Enterprise Linux 8 - AppStream  enabled: 4,637
InstallMedia-BaseOS            Red Hat Enterprise Linux 8 - BaseOS     enabled: 1,658
[root@redhat1 ~]# yum-config-manager --disable InstallMedia-AppStream
Updating Subscription Management repositories.
Unable to read consumer identity
This system is not registered to Red Hat Subscription Management. You can use subscriptio
n-manager to register.
[root@redhat1 ~]# yum repolist all
Updating Subscription Management repositories.
Unable to read consumer identity
This system is not registered to Red Hat Subscription Management. You can use subscriptio
n-manager to register.
Last metadata expiration check: 0:01:15 ago on Sat 09 Nov 2019 10:18:34 AM +04.
repo id                        repo name                              status
InstallMedia-AppStream         Red Hat Enterprise Linux 8 - AppStream  disabled
InstallMedia-BaseOS            Red Hat Enterprise Linux 8 - BaseOS     enabled: 1,660
[root@redhat1 ~]#
```

Enable a repository

```
# yum-config-manager --enable InstallMedia-AppStream
```

```
[root@redhat1 ~]# yum-config-manager --enable InstallMedia-AppStream
Updating Subscription Management repositories.
Unable to read consumer identity
This system is not registered to Red Hat Subscription Management. You can use subscriptio
n-manager to register.
[root@redhat1 ~]# yum repolist all
Updating Subscription Management repositories.
Unable to read consumer identity
This system is not registered to Red Hat Subscription Management. You can use subscriptio
n-manager to register.
Last metadata expiration check: 0:11:25 ago on Sat 09 Nov 2019 10:18:34 AM +04.
repo id                    repo name                                    status
InstallMedia-AppStream     Red Hat Enterprise Linux 8 - AppStream       enabled: 4,637
InstallMedia-BaseOS        Red Hat Enterprise Linux 8 - BaseOS          enabled: 1,658
[root@redhat1 ~]#
```

Add repository

Repositories usually provide their own .repo file for repository configuration. To add repository which provides .repo file you can use this command

Syntax

```
# yum-config-manager --add-repo repository_url
```

Example

```
# yum-config-manager --add-repo https://www.example.com/abc.repo
```

CodeReady Linux Builder Repository

Redhat provides BaseOS and Appstream repos by default in all type of subscriptions, both repositories are enabled by default. In addition to the BaseOS and Appstream repos, a new repository CodeReady has been added for developers. All subscriptions include access to the new CodeReady Linux Builder repository. As the name implies, CodeReady Linux Builder is for developers who develop linux application using Red Hat Enterprise Linux infrastructure. It includes packages specifically for developers to use when building their applications. CodeReady Linux Builder is repository similar to optional repository found in the previous version of Redhat enterprise Linux. the CodeReady Linux Builder contains build tooling and -devel packages. Although Red Hat provides updates and maintain contents in CodeReady Linux Builder during the life of Red Hat Enterprise Linux 8, but packages in CodeReady Linux Builder are not supported by RedHat. Therefore Developers are encouraged to use the content for application building purpose only and should use with caution in production environment. The example of additional packages can be additional libraries for perl which are not commonly used.

Enabling the Repository

To enable the repository, you can use **subscription-manager** command:

```
# subscription-manager repos --enable codeready-builder-for-rhel-8-x86_64-rpms
```

To list the modules of codeready-builder repository

```
yum module list --disablerepo=* --enablerepo=codeready-builder-for-rhel-8-x86_64-rpms
```

Enable third party repository

As redhat is open source project there is very few limitation for availability of software. If software you require is not available in the BaseOS, Appstream and codeready repository you can install third party repositories which provide required software. The reason for non-availability of the software can be the license issues. These third party repositories can be added in many ways. One way is to install repo file other is to create own repo file and third way is to install the rpm package supplied by the repository site for adding repository. Simple example for requirement of third party repository can be proprietary codecs, software which do not adhere GPL and open source license. For demonstration purpose we will install third party repository Extra Packages for Enterprise Linux (or EPEL) repository which is maintained by Fedora Special Interest Group. Installing and enabling

81

EPEL repository is very simple in RHEL. Use yum command to install package epel-release

```
# yum install https://dl.fedoraproject.org/pub/epel/epel-release-latest-8.noarch.rpm
```

Now check it

```
# yum repolist enabled
```

When you using EPEL repository it is advisable to enable codeready repository as some software may have dependences in the codeready. Other than EPEL there are other very famous third party repositories are there like rpmfusion, REMI, ELRepo, NUX-dextop etc.

Manually adding repository

As mentioned earlier you can also add repository by manually creating repo file. Repository configuration files for yum repositories are located in `/etc/yum.repos.d/` directory having .repo extension. This repository configuration file has following options :-

repo file

Repository ID	One word unique repository ID
Name	Human readable string describing the repository
Baseurl	URL to the repodata directory of repository is located.
Gpgcheck	Enable/disable GPG signature checking
Gpgkey	URL to the GPG key file for a repository
Exclude	List of the packages to exclude
Includepkgs	List of packages that yum can see
Enabled	Enable/Disable repository

Minimum required fields are:

- Repository ID
- Name
- Baseurl
- Enabled

Example

```
[cr]
name=CentOS-$releasever - cr
baseurl=http://mirror.centos.org/centos/$releasever/cr/$basearch/
gpgcheck=1
gpgkey=file:///etc/pki/rpm-gpg/RPM-GPG-KEY-CentOS-7
enabled=0
```

DVD ISO as YUM Repository

When you are using Redhat servers in production environment there are four ways to install the additional software.

1. Server has internet access so it can install software from RedHat web repositories.
2. You have your own satellite server which provides the content.
3. Using downloaded ISO image
4. Directory as repository.

In the procedure bellow we will explain the scenario where your server doesn't have internet and satellite server connection.

You can make downloaded RHEL ISO image as repository in three ways. If you have DVD drive in the server. you can write the image to DVD and use this DVD drive to copy the content to local directory so in case you remove the DVD still repository will work. Other scenario can be you have ISO image and the server is a virtual machine you can attach the ISO image to the server. Third scenario which I generally use is that I will transfer the ISO file to the server and loop mount the

ISO image so that its contents are available as repository. I will explain the third scenario but the procedure is almost same for all three scenarios, the repository directory must have contents it doesn't matter how you copy the contents.

Steps are bellow:-

1. Download the ISO image
2. Transfer the image to the target server using scp or FTP. In this example ISO had already been transferred to the server in /disc directory
3. Make Directory for mounting the ISO image. This directory will be used as repository.

```
# mkdir /rhcd
```

4. Mount RHEL DVD ISO

   Syntax

```
mount -o loop /path_to_iso  /mount_point
Example
```

```
# mount -o loop /disc/RHEL8.iso /rhcd
```

5. Create .repo repository configuration file with following content . If you are coming from old version of RedHat there is change in RedHat version 8, now you have to define two repositories instead of one which are BaseOS and Appstream

```
# vi /etc/yum.repos.d/rhiso.repo
```

```
[InstallMedia-BaseOS]
name=Red Hat Enterprise Linux 8 - BaseOS
metadata_expire=-1
gpgcheck=1
enabled=1
```

```
baseurl=file:///rhcd/BaseOS/
gpgkey=file:///etc/pki/rpm-gpg/RPM-GPG-KEY-redhat-release

[InstallMedia-AppStream]
name=Red Hat Enterprise Linux 8 - AppStream
metadata_expire=-1
gpgcheck=1
enabled=1
baseurl=file:///rhcd/AppStream/
gpgkey=file:///etc/pki/rpm-gpg/RPM-GPG-KEY-redhat-release
```

Clean the yum cache

```
# yum clean all
```

Now list the repositories

```
# yum repolist
```

Own Custom Repository

There are cases when you require to create your own repository. For example you have developed a software and it is in rpm format for distribution or you may have downloaded some set of software which you want to distribute through repository. To make your own custom repository for RPM packages the steps are following :-

1. Create directory for your custom repository.

```
mkdir /myrepo
```

2. Transfer/ download files to this directory
3. Use **createrepo** to create repodata. If createrepo command is not there than first install createrepo command. createrepo is provided by the createrepo_c package.

```
# yum -y install createrepo_c
```

```
# createrepo /myrepo
```

4. Create configuration files

   /etc/yum.repos.d/mycustom.repo

   Below is example of custom repo file

```
[mycustomrepo]
name=Custom Repository
baseurl=file:///myrepo/
enabled=1
gpgcheck=0
```

Chapter 9.

Managing services

When system boot, it starts and stops some services to achieve required state of the system. Suppose you want to start the system in GUI mode, system has to start all the services related to Desktop environment. Same way if you have configured the server as web server you have to start the web services during boot process. Even to do its basic tasks it requires many services to be running like network, date and time etc. In the older versions of Redhat enterprise Linux **SysV** was the default service manager. **SysV** use to start services one by one at boot time this means next service will start once previous service finish starting. In RHEL version 7 Systemd was introduced.

Introduction to systemd

Systemd is a system and service manager for RHEL 8. It has limited backward compatible with SysV init scripts. It provides number of new features like:-

- Parallel startup of system service at boot time
- On demand activation of devices
- Dependency based service control logic
- Path-based activation: on demand activation of services when a particular file or directory changes its state
- Device based activation (like USB)
- Earlier BOOT Logging

Before systemd, previous versions of RHEL used SysV scripts located in the **/etc/rc.d/init.d/** directory to control the system state. With

Systemd these init scripts have been replaced with service units, service units reside in **/etc/systemd/system/** directory. Service units end with the **.service** file extension. **systemctl** command is used to view, start, stop, restart, enable, or disable system services. If you are coming from Redhat version 6 or earlier there use to be more than one command for service management, like for service status management **service** command and for service startup management **chkconfig** command. With Systemd it has been replaced by single command **systemctl**. Now systemctl command can handle both service management and its startup at boot.

Systemd unit files locations

Detail	Command
/usr/lib/systemd/system/	Systemd unit files initially get installed here.
/run/systemd/system/	At run time Systemd unit files are created. here This directory takes precedence over the directory with installed service unit files.
/etc/systemd/system/	When you enable a service Systemd unit files created here as well as unit files added for extending a service. This directory takes precedence over the directory with runtime unit files.

Service Status Management

Detail	Command

Starts a service	`systemctl start `*`name`*`.service`
	
	Example
	
	`systemctl start iscsi.service`

Stops a service	`systemctl stop `*`name`*`.service`
	
	Example
	
	`systemctl stop iscsi.service`

Restarts a service	`systemctl restart name.service`
	
	Example
	
	`systemctl restart iscsi.service`

Restarts a service only if it is running.	`systemctl try-restart`
	`name.service`
	
	Example
	
	`systemctl try-restart iscsi.service`

Reloads configuration	`systemctl reload `*`name`*`.service`
	
	Example
	
	`systemctl reload iscsi.service`

Checks if a service is running.	`systemctl status `*`name`*`.service`
	`systemctl is-active `*`name`*`.service`
	
	Example
	
	`systemctl status iscsi.service`
	`systemctl is-active iscsi.service`

Displays the status of all service	`systemctl list-units --type service --all`
	or
	`systemctl -at service`

89

Like **chkconfig** in earlier versions, you can use the **systemctl** to control the services during system boot.

Enable and disable service at startup

Task	Command

Enable service	`systemctl enable name.service`
	
	Example
	
	`systemctl enable iscsi.service`

Disable service	`systemctl disable name.service`
	
	Example
	
	`systemctl disable iscsi.service`

To prevent service from starting dynamically or even manually unless unmasked	`systemctl mask name.service`
	
	Example
	
	`systemctl mask iscsi.service`

Check whether a service enabled or not	`systemctl is-enabled name.service`
	
	Example
	
	`systemctl is-enabled iscsi.service`

Lists all services and check if they are enabled or not	`systemctl list-unit-files --type service`

Service unit information

When we give command `systemctl -status name.service`. It provides following information

Field	Description
Loaded	Whether the service unit is loaded, the absolute path to the unit file, whether the unit is enabled.

90

Active	Running or not
Main PID	PID of the service
Process	Information about process
CGroup	information about Control Groups.

Example

```
# [root@redhat1 ~]# systemctl status atd.service
• atd.service - Job spooling tools
   Loaded: loaded (/usr/lib/systemd/system/atd.service; enabled;
vendor preset:>
   Active: active (running) since Sun 2019-11-10 14:13:03 +04; 3min
42s ago
 Main PID: 1077 (atd)
    Tasks: 1 (limit: 23864)
   Memory: 664.0K
   CGroup: /system.slice/atd.service
           └─1077 /usr/sbin/atd -f
Nov 10 14:13:03 redhat1 systemd[1]: Started Job spooling tools.
```

Managing services

To list all services and their status

```
# systemctl -at service
```

To list current setting of specific service

Syntax

```
systemctl status name.service
```

Example

```
# systemctl status httpd.service
```

Enable service

Syntax

```
systemctl enable name.service
```

Example

```
# systemctl enable iscsi.service
```

Disable service

Syntax

```
systemctl disable name.service
```

Example

```
# systemctl disable iscsi.service
```

Determine status of service

Syntax

```
# systemctl status name.service
```

Example

```
# systemctl status httpdd.service
```

Starting service

Syntax

```
# systemctl start name.service
```

Example

```
# systemctl start httpd.service
```

Stopping service

Syntax

```
# systemctl stop name.service
```

Example

```
# systemctl stop httpd.service
```

Restarting service

Syntax

```
# systemctl restart name.service
```

Example

```
# systemctl restart httpd.service
```

Install new service

Procedure to install new service

1. Install new service package

```
# yum install service_name
```

2. Configure the service to start automatically at startup

```
# systemctl enable name.service
```

3. Start the service

```
# systemctl start name.service
```

Example

```
# yum install httpd
# systemctl enable httpd.service
# systemctl start httpd.service
```

systemd Targets

Older versions like RedHat 6 and earlier implemented run levels. Run level is state or mode of OS in which it will run. Each run level causes certain number of services to be stopped or started, providing control over behavior of machine. However, in RHEL 7 it was replaced by **systemd targets.** There were seven **Runlevels** in redhat 6 or earlier, which has been replaced by corresponding **target units** in new version

Run level	Description	Target unit
0	Halt the machine	poweroff.target
1	Single user mode	rescue.target
2	Multiuser with command line no GUI	multiuser.target
3	Multiuser with command line no GUI	multiuser.target
4	Multiuser with command line no GUI	multiuser.target
5	Multiuser with GUI	graphical.target
6	Reboot	reboot.target

List currently loaded target

```
# systemctl list-units --type target
```

Default Target

Default target decides the direction in which **systemd** process takes the system at boot time. The file **/etc/inittab** is no longer used to set the default run level as it was in earlier version of RHEL. Now default target unit is represented by the **/etc/systemd/system/default.target** file. This file is a symbolic link to current set target. Suppose current

94

target is set to graphical, this file will be symbolic link to graphical target file

Change default target

Syntax

```
# systemctl set-default <name of target>.target
```

Example

```
# systemctl set-default graphical.target
Removed symlink /etc/systemd/system/default.target.
Created symlink from /etc/systemd/system/default.target to
/usr/lib/systemd/system/graphical.target.
```

Viewing the Default Target

```
# systemctl get-default
```

Changing the Current Target

After changing default target, the current target remains unchanged until next reboot. To change the current target without reboot use

Syntax

```
# systemctl isolate default
```

Or

```
# systemctl default
```

To Change the current target to different target other than default target. Suppose you want to start the single user target

Syntax

```
# systemctl isolate newtarget.target
```

Example

```
# systemctl isoloate rescue.target
```

## Chapter 10

OpenSSH

SSH(Secure Shell) provides a secure channel over insecure network in client server architecture. SSH is a replacement of telnet, which is insecure protocol. It allows secure channel to login and execute command remotely because all communication between client and server is encrypted. RHEL includes the OpenSSH package for ssh. The OpenSSH suite comes with RHEL is SSH version 2. OpenSSH provides number of tools for secure communication like ssh, scp and sftp. It also offers capabilities for secure tunneling, different authentication methods, and easy configuration. RHEL 8 includes **openssh**, **openssh-server** and **openssh-clients** packages. The openssh package also requires openssl-libs to be installed on the system, as it provides cryptographic libraries for encrypted communication. The default installation of RHEL comes with openssh preinstalled. If is not there, you need to install them with this command.

```
# yum install openssh openssh-server openssh-clients openssl-libs
```

Start the service

```
# systemctl start sshd.service
```

Enable the service to start automatically on system boot

```
# systemctl enable sshd.service
```

Check the status

```
# systemctl status sshd.service
```

Versions of SSH protocol

There are two varieties of SSH ,version 1 and version 2. The OpenSSH suite comes under RHEL 8 is SSH version 2. SSH2 is a more secure, also includes SFTP, which is functionally similar to FTP, but with encryption. scp instead of rcp.

To check version of ssh you are running

```
# ssh -v localhost
```

This command show verbose mode of ssh in that look for following line

```
debug1: Local version string SSH-2.0-OpenSSH_7.8
```

Configuration file

File	Description
/etc/ssh/sshd_config	The default configuration file for the sshd daemon
/etc/ssh/ssh_config	The default configuration file for SSH client. it will be overridden, if **~/.ssh/config** exists
~/.ssh/config	The client-side configuration file

Connecting from client

If you are on the Linux client machine and you want to login on to remote RHEL server you require ssh client installed on your client machine and SSH server running on RHEL server. From client give this command

```
$ ssh -x user@server-IPaddress_or_hostname
```

Example

```
$ ssh -x root@RHEL1
```

97

```
The authenticity of host 'RHEL1 (192.168.131.152)' can't be
established.
ECDSA key fingerprint is
SHA256:kJkcVAsgMdv5FsbEeaHWNK33LJHHLaHSUC8WZE/Sri8.
Are you sure you want to continue connecting (yes/no)? yes
Warning: Permanently added 'RHEL1,192.168.131.152' (ECDSA) to
the list of known hosts.
root@RHEL1's password:
[root@RHEL1 ~]
```

It will ask password of the user name specified in the ssh command. When ssh connection from client to server is made first time, the public key of server is stored locally on the client, so it's identity can be verified next time.

Ctrl + d or **exit** command will terminate **ssh** session.

To connect MS windows client to RHEL server you require third party software like **putty**.

ssh keys
ssh keys helps in identifying yourself to a server using public key cryptography and challenge response authentication. ssh keys are generated in pairs known, one as public and other as private key. The public is for sharing and private key is for you. It must be kept safely. Server having public key can send challenge, which can only be answered by client holding private key. This allows password less login.

Passwordless Login Using SSH Keys

SSH also allows to connect trusted SSH client to SSH server without password. In this section, we will learn how to do passwordless login from Linux client to Linux server. In bellow example, **RHEL1** is Linux client and **RHEL2** act as Linux server.

1. Create keys on **RHEL1** host

```
[root@RHEL1 ~]# ssh-keygen
```

2. Copy public key from **RHEL1** to second server **RHEL2** host

```
# scp ~/.ssh/id_rsa.pub root@RHEL2:/root/id_rsa.server1.pub
```

3. On second server **RHEL2** create directory .ssh in the home directory in our case the user is root its home directory is /root and change the permissions to **700** (only owner can read, write and execute) .

```
[root@RHEL2 ~]# mkdir .ssh
[root@RHEL2 ~]# chmod 700 .ssh
```

4. Append the public key earlier copied in /root directory file to **authorized_keys** file and change permissions.

```
[root@RHEL2 ~]# cat id_rsa.server1.pub >> .ssh/authorized_keys
[root@RHEL2 ~]# chmod 644 .ssh/authorized_keys
```

5. Now try login from **RHEL1** to server **RHEL2** it will not ask for password.

```
[root@RHEL1 ~]# ssh root@RHEL2
```

scp Utility

scp is part of openssh suit which can be used to transfer files between machines over a encrypted connection. It is secure alternative to rcp command. Syntax for scp command is :-

Syntax

```
scp filename username@hostname:/directory
```

Example

```
RHEL1~]$ scp abc.txt user1@RHEL2:.
```

In this example we will transfer abc.txt from host1 ie. **RHEL1** to remote machine **RHEL2**.

To transfer a file from remote machine to the local system

 Syntax:

```
scp username@hostname:remotefile localdirectory
```

Example

In this example we will transfer xyz.txt from remote host2 ie. RHEL2 to local machine RHEL1. On RHEL1 shell prompt

```
RHEL1~]$ scp user2@RHEL2:/home/user2/xyz.txt /home/user1/.
```

sftp Utility

File Transfer Protocol (FTP) is widely used protocol for transferring files between computers specially for downloading files from internet. However, it uses unencrypted communication, which is not secure. SSH File Transfer Protocol (SFTP) is a SSH implementation for FTP that provides encrypted data transfer. sftp provides interactive prompt. You can use command to download or upload file to remote host.

To connect to a remote system using **sftp username@hostname or IP address** of server it will ask the password for username

Syntax

```
sftp username@hostname
```

Example

```
# sftp user1@RHEL2
```

```
[user1@centos1 ~]$
[user1@centos1 ~]$ sftp user1@centos2
The authenticity of host 'centos2 (192.168.131.152)' can't be established.
ECDSA key fingerprint is 30:ab:8c:ec:38:aa:36:80:b9:4d:c5:dc:01:ff:00:bf.
Are you sure you want to continue connecting (yes/no)? yes
Warning: Permanently added 'centos2,192.168.131.152' (ECDSA) to the list of known hosts.
user1@centos2's password:
Connected to centos2.
sftp>
```

Common Commands for sftp

Command	Description
?	help
ls	List the content of remote directory
lls	List the content of local directory
cd	Change the remote directory
lcd	Change local directory
mkdir *directoryname*	Make directory at remote server
lmdir *directoryname*	Make local directory
rmdir *directoryname*	Remove remote directory
put *filename*	Transfer file to remote server
mput files	Transfer multiple files to remote machine
get *filename*	Download file to local machine
mget files	Download multiple files
bye	Quite sftp
! command	Run shell command

Examples

Getting help

```
sftp> ?
Available commands:
bye                      Quit sftp
cd path                  Change remote directory to 'path'
chgrp grp path           Change group of file 'path' to 'grp'
[...output truncated.. ]
```

Uploading single file

Transferring file from local to remote machine

```
sftp> put xyz.txt
Uploading xyz.txt to /home/user1/xyz.txt
xyz.txt                      100% 1508      1.5KB/s   00:00
```

Uploading multiple files

```
sftp> mput *.txt
Uploading 11.txt to /home/user1/11.txt
11.txt                       100% 1663      1.6KB/s   00:00
Uploading a2.txt to /home/user1/a2.txt
a2.txt                       100% 1715      1.7KB/s   00:00
```

Downloading single file

Transfer file from remote to local machine

```
sftp> get abc.txt
Fetching /home/user1/abc.txt to abc.txt
/home/user1/abc.txt          100% 1508      1.5KB/s   00:00
```

Downloading multiple files

```
sftp> mget *.txt
```

Changing Directories

To change from one directory to another directory

On remote machine.

```
sftp> cd Documents
```

On Local machine

```
sftp> lcd Downloads
```

Create new Directory

On remote Machine

```
sftp> mkdir julli
```

On local Machine

```
sftp> lmkdir David
```

Remove Directories

```
sftp> rmdir julli
```

Exit sFTP

```
sftp> bye
```

## Chapter 11

VNC

VNC Virtual Network Computing is graphical desktop sharing system. It is used to get GUI desktop of Linux server remotely. In VNC there two parts, one is VNC server other is VNC client. VNC server runs on RHEL server and client runs on MS Windows or Linux workstation. X Server runs on RHEL server where as VNC client shows only copy of the display.

To configure VNC on server whose desktop you want to share

1. install

```
# yum install tigervnc-server
```

2. Set VNC password

Syntax

```
su - user_name
vncpasswd
```

Example

```
[root@redhat1 ~]# su - admin
[admin@redhat1 ~]$ vncpasswd
Password:
Verify:
Would you like to enter a view-only password (y/n)? n
A view-only password is not used
[admin@redhat1 ~]$ █
```

3. create file **/etc/systemd/system/vncserver@.service**

```
# vi /etc/systemd/system/vncserver@.service
```

Add following lines in this file. Make sure replace user name, group and home directory with appropriate user and home directory whose password you had set I the last step.

```
[Unit]
Description=Remote Desktop VNC Service
After=syslog.target network.target

[Service]
Type=forking
WorkingDirectory=/home/admin
User=admin
Group=admin

ExecStartPre=/bin/sh -c '/usr/bin/vncserver -kill %i > /dev/null 2>&1 || :'
ExecStart=/usr/bin/vncserver -autokill %i
ExecStop=/usr/bin/vncserver -kill %i

[Install]
WantedBy=multi-user.target
```

4. Start and enable the VNC service on display number as 1

```
# systemctl start vncserver@:1.service
# systemctl enable vncserver@:1.service
```

5. Verify whether VNC server is listening at 5901

```
netstat -tunlp | grep 5901
ss -tunlp | grep 5901
```

Open the Firewall ports

```
firewall-cmd --permanent --add-port=5901/tcp
firewall-cmd --reload
```

6. Download vncviewer from tigervnc site on the windows 7 /10 workstation

7. Run the downloaded file, it will prompt for server IP address and display number of vnc server. After writing IP address and display number in format `IPAddress:DisplayNumber`, press connect.

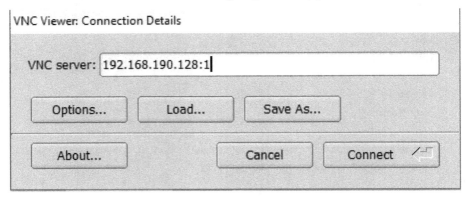

8. It will prompt for password. Provide the password you had set with vncpasswd command.

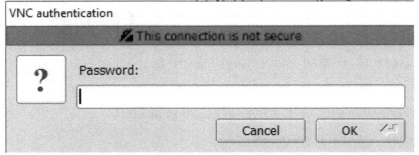

9. Now you will see the server screen.

## Chapter 12

Web server

In this online world almost all information is no the web, this information can be accessed by means of various websites. To run these website requires a server known as webserver. A webserver is program, which allows web browser clients to access website pages. It uses HTTP (Hypertext Transfer Protocol). In RHEL 8 Apache HTTP server can be used as Web Server.

Deploying http server

Installation of Apache web server includes following steps
1. Installation
2. Start service
3. Enable the service to start at boot time
4. Firewall configuration
5. Test

Install http server

```
# yum install httpd
```

Start service

```
# systemctl start httpd
```

Enable the service to start on boot

```
# systemctl enable httpd
```

Open firewall port and reload its configuration

```
# firewall-cmd --permanent --add-service=http
# firewall-cmd --reload
```

Default directory where http keeps contents

/var/www/html

Configuration file

/etc/httpd/conf/httpd.conf

Directory for additional configuration files that are included in the main configuration file.

/etc/httpd/conf.d/

Verifying Configuration

After changing configuration, verify it before using:-

```
# apachectl configtest
```

If you change the configuration files, you have to restart/reload the service, for that refer the **Restarting service** section.

Test

1. Create file in directory /var/www/html/index.html and Write **Hello**

2. Save the file and exit

3. Open the Firefox and on the address bar write http://localhost

4. You should see hello

Stop the Service

To stop running httpd service

```
# systemctl stop httpd
```

To prevent http service from starting automatically at boot time

```
# systemctl disable httpd
```

Restarting service

There are three ways to restart the service httpd

1. Complete restart using systemctl command

```
# systemctl restart httpd
```

2. Reload only configuration, in case you have changed the configuration. In this case, all request during reload will be denied including active requests also.

```
# systemctl reload httpd
```

3. To reload configuration without affecting active requests. If the daemon is not running, it is started.

```
# apachectl gracefull
```

Verifying the service

To verify the service if it is active

```
# systemctl is-active httpd
```

Virtual Hosts

The Apache HTTP Server offers option to create multiple websites on single webserver using virtual hosts. Based on host name, IP address or port number, virtual hosts allow same webserver to provide different information. You can host multiple websites on a single machine with a single IP using virtual hosting. Virtual hosting is suitable for shared web hosting environments, where multiple websites are hosted on a single server.

Steps to host multiple sites on single server using virtual hosting:-

1. Create the directory structure
2. Create test web pages for each host
3. Set ownership and permissions
4. Change SELinux context of files
5. Configure your virtual host directories
6. Change the Apache configuration file
7. Create virtual host configuration files
8. Verify the configuration files and restart the httpd service
9. Create DNS record in /etc/hosts file or in the DNS server
10. Test the virtual hosts

Steps in detail

In this example, we will host two websites abc_example.com and xyz_example.com.

1. Create Directory Structure

First, create directory for each website to hold html files. This directory is known as document root for each website

```
# mkdir -p /var/www/html/abc_example.com
# mkdir -p /var/www/html/xyz_example.com
```

2. Create test web pages for each host

```
# vi /var/www/html/abc_example.com/index.html
```

Add following content

```
Abc_example.com
```

Save the file and exit from vi

Same way

```
# vi /var/www/html/xyz_example.com/index.html
```

Add following content

```
Xyz_example.com
```

Save the file and exit from vi

3. Set ownership and permissions

Set the ownership of newly created directories to apache user and group

```
# chown -R apache:apache /var/www/html/abc_example.com
# chown -R apache:apache /var/www/html/xyz_example.com
```

Change the /var/www/html folder readable by world

```
# chmod -R 755 /var/www/html
```


4. Change SELinux context of files

If SELinux is enabled in the system change context of newly created directories.

```
# semanage fcontext -a -t httpd_sys_content_t
"/var/www/html/abc_example.com(/.*)?"
# semanage fcontext -a -t httpd_sys_content_t
"/var/www/html/xyz_example.com(/.*)?"
# restorecon -R -v /var/www/html/
```

Verify the context

```
# ls -laZ /var/www/html/
```

5. Configure your virtual host configuration directories

Create two directories for configuration files for virtual sites one directory is for all configured websites (sites-available) and another to hold symbolic links to virtual hosts that will be published (sites-enabled).

```
# mkdir -p /etc/httpd/sites-available
# mkdir -p /etc/httpd/sites-enabled
```

6. Change Apache configuration file

Edit the main configuration file (/etc/httpd/conf/httpd.conf) to include new configuration directory (sites-enabled) so that Apache will look for virtual hosts in this directory.

```
# vi /etc/httpd/conf/httpd.conf
```

Add this line at the very end of the file:
```
IncludeOptional sites-enabled/*.conf
```
Save the file and exit from vi

7. Create virtual host configuration files

Create configuration files for each virtual host

```
# vi /etc/httpd/sites-available/abc_example.com.conf
```
```
<VirtualHost *:80>
    ServerName www.abc_example.com
    ServerAlias abc_example.com
    DocumentRoot /var/www/html/abc_example.com
```

```
</VirtualHost>
```

```
# vi /etc/httpd/sites-available/xyz_example.com.conf
```

```
<VirtualHost *:80>
    ServerName www.xyz_example.com
    ServerAlias xyz_example.com
    DocumentRoot /var/www/html/xyz_example.com
</VirtualHost>
```

Create soft links of virtual host configuration files in **sites-enabled** directory (Note this command is in single line, due to page width limitation it wrapped to next line. When you issue this command, issue it in single line)

```
# ln -s /etc/httpd/sites-available/abc_example.com.conf
/etc/httpd/sites-enabled/abc_example.com.conf
```

```
# ln -s /etc/httpd/sites-available/xyz_example.com.conf
/etc/httpd/sites-enabled/xyz_example.com.conf
```

8. Verify the configuration files and restart the httpd service

Verify the configuration files

```
# apachectl configtest
```

Restart Service

```
# systemctl restart httpd
```

6. Create DNS record in /etc/hosts file or in the DNS server

If you have DNS server you can add the entries for

113

```
www.abc_example.com
www.xyz_example.com
```

For testing purpose you can add the entries in /etc/hosts

```
vi /etc/hosts
```

```
192.168.131.152    www.abc_example.com
192.168.131.152    www.zyz_example.com
```

7. Test the new websites (virtual hosts)

Open your web browser on RHEL Server in GUI Mode and go to the URLs

http://www.abc_example.com

and

http://www.xyz_example.com.

You will see the content of each website

Chapter 13.

Exploring Shell

Shell

A shell is a command-line interpreter. It is interface between user and Operating system. User gives command on Shell prompt and operating system executes that command. As shell is a command language interpreter, the basic purpose of shell is to translate human readable commands typed at a terminal into system actions. A shell is a special user program through which other programs are invoked. The shell gets started when the user logs in or start the terminal. Although several shells are available with Linux distributions like Bash, Korn, C shell zsh etc, Bash is the default shell for Linux. Depending on the shell you use, there may be minor difference in command's usage.

Shell Script

Generally, we use shell in interactive mode, where user inputs command and gets output. However, some time you use shell scripts. Shell script is script you write to give series of command. Scripts that are more complex check conditions and run loops. Seasoned administrators use shell scripts to automate administrative tasks and to monitor system. Suppose, you want to check the disk space, memory availability and environment variables before invoking a program. There are two ways to do it, either you can give all commands manually every time before running that program or you can use shell script to do that. Shell scripts generally end with **sh** extension. Figure bellow shows an example of shell script.

```
user@Mylinux ~ $
user@Mylinux ~ $ cat /usr/share/doc/acpid/examples/ac.sh
#!/bin/sh
# /etc/acpid/ac.sh
# Detect loss of AC power and regaining of AC power, and take action
# appropriatly.

# On my laptop anyway, this script doesn't not get different parameters for
# loss of power and regained power. So, I have to use a separate program to
# tell what the adapter status is.

# This uses the spicctrl program for probing the sonvpi device.
BACKLIGHT=$(spicctrl -B)

if on ac power; then
        # Now on AC power.

        # Tell longrun to go crazy.
        longrun -f performance
        longrun -s 0 100

        # Turn up the backlight unless it's up far enough.
        if [ "$BACKLIGHT" -lt 108 ]; then
                spicctrl -b 108
        fi
else
        # Now off AC power.

        # Tell longrun to be a miser.
        longrun -f economy
        longrun -s 0 50 # adjust to suite..

        # Don't allow the screen to be too bright, but don't turn the
        # backlight  up  on removal, and don't turn it all the way down, as
        # that is unusable on my laptop in most conditions. Adjust to
        # taste.
        if [ "$BACKLIGHT" -gt 68 ]; then
                spicctrl -b 68
        fi
fi
user@Mylinux ~ $ ▮
```

Command line Interface

Command line interface (CLI) is way to access the shell. If you do
RHEL installation without GUI or Minimal, you will get only command
line interface through virtual terminals. When you install Linux with GUI
you have two option to access CLI

- Virtual Terminals
- Graphical Terminal

Virtual Terminals

Virtual Terminal is full screen command line interface. If you are
working on RHEL server locally, you will get more than one Virtual
terminal running on same server. Having more than one virtual terminal
allows the administrator to switch to another terminal if necessary.
Even with Graphical Desktop environment installed you can access
virtual terminals. Virtual terminals can be accessed by pressing

116

Ctrl+Alt+F2 till F6. To come back to the graphical session, press Ctrl+Alt+F1. On pressing Ctrl+Alt+F2 you will get first Virtual terminal like that

```
Red Hat Enterprise Linux 8.0 (Ootpa)
Kernel 4.18.0-80.el8.x86_64 on an x86_64

Activate the web console with: systemctl enable --now cockpit.socket

redhat1 login: _
```

Login and start issuing commands

Graphical Terminal Emulator

System with Graphical desktop environment can get CLI inside GUI with **Terminal Emulator.** Terminal allows you to open a window and lets you interact with the shell. Depending on Graphical Desktop environment installed on Linux distributions you have bunch of terminal emulator available like gnome-terminal, konsole, rxvt, xterm, LXterminal, guake, terminator, tilde, yakuake etc. Gnome-terminal is the default terminal emulator for RHEL Linux with GNOME desktop

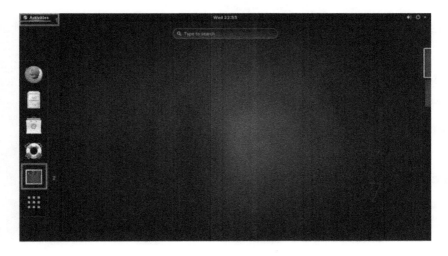

environment. To start Gnome terminal, press Activities and press terminal icon.

Command prompt

Although you can customize the prompt, but more often you will get either # or $ at end of prompt. Where # indicates the user is logged in as root (administrator) user and $ prompt as normal user. You can display additional information in the prompt like username, current directory and server name even you can show current date and time.

Structure of commands

Normally if you run command from the shell prompt will have the following format:

```
command -options <filename>
```

Example

```
tail -f myfile
```

However, file name is not used in all commands. in some commands only command or command with options are used

```
ls -la
```

Tips for the bash shell

Whether you are on virtual terminal or using Terminal emulator, command format is same. Following are some of the useful features of bash shell you can use in day-to-day tasks

TAB completion

Tab completion is one of the most useful feature of Bash shell. It has ability to guess the command, directory or file name by pressing TAB

118

after writing partial command, directory or file name, shell will automatically complete the word if only one option is present otherwise it will offers all possible completions. For example, suppose you want to change directory to **abc** you write **cd ab** and press TAB, the system will complete the word automatically.

Bash History

Shell saves all the command given by you on shell prompt in a file in your home directory. You can check the last commands by giving **history** command.

```
$ history
```

If you want to give last command again, you can press UP arrow key and then press **ENTER** key. You can press **UP** arrow key repeatedly to scroll backward in the history of commands.

Wildcards

Wildcards or wild characters are symbols representing one or more characters in the shell command. Most common wild card characters are

*   Star

?   Question mark

[ ]   Square baskets

Where

Star (*)

Represents zero or more characters

Example

```
$ ls b*
```

List all files starting with b

Question mark (?)

Represents single character

Example

```
$ ls ?at
```

List all files whose first letter of file name can be any character like bat, cat or hat

Square brackets

Represent a range of characters

Example

ls b[1-5]

List all files starting with b and second character should be numeric character starting from 1 to 5. It can b1, b2, b3, b4 and b5

Check the current shell

```
# echo $SHELL
```

## Chapter 14

Backup and Restore

Backup of your computer data is always important to prevent data loss. Backup saves you in case of data loss. There can be many reasons for data loss like hard disk failure, OS failure, virus, malware or due to human error. Before taking actual backup you should try to answer three W's : what, when and where

What

In my experience as an administrator if you ask any user what part of data is important for backup, the simple, answer will be whole data. As an administrator, you should understand it is ideal to take backup of whole system daily but practically, first you require huge device which can accommodate the whole data. Second taking backup also takes time. Suppose if you take full backup of server which is online, it may takes hours to finish. In this case, by the time you are on verge of finishing the backup half of the data has already changed. Therefore, data insistency arises. Best way to take consistent data backup is to stop the whole system and then take backup but if your backup window is large, then it is very difficult to get down time of production systems. The solution for this problem is to segregate the data in to two or more parts. First part of data that is changing regularly. Second, the data that changes once a while. The best example of that is, in normal production environment you have software binary files that changes very rarely and data files which gets updated regularly. You can take backup of whole system monthly or quarterly and take backup of data files daily.

Where

Next question is where you want to keep backup. There two part of this question first part is device on which you want to take backup. It can be external hard disk, tape drive, DVD or even USB drive. The second part of question is the location where you want to physically keep the backup media. It can be stored at same location (**onsite**) or at remote location (**offsite**). The benefit of storing at same location is easy and quick availability in case of loss of data but when there is total loss of site in case of flood , hurricane or fire ,offsite backup is more useful. According to the best practices, you should follow 3-2-1 plan. In this, you keep three backup copies of your data two copies onsite and third copy offsite. If condition arises, in which you require backup copy to restore data you have two good copies of data onsite and in case of total disaster, remote copy is there.

When

Next question, when to take backup? It all depends on your business needs. Frequency of data backup depends on frequency of change and criticality of data. Next thing, which define backup time, is functionality of system. System used for server and system used as workstation can have different backup windows.

Backup type

Now you know the answer of three W's, its time to understand backup more deeply. Backup is broadly of three types depending on how much backup you are taking.
1. Full backup
2. Differential backup

3. Incremental backup

Full backup

As name suggest it is backup which contains all files. When you require to restore only one full backup is required.

Differential backup

A differential backup is cumulative backup of files, which have changed since last full backup. In case of restore only last full backup and last differential backup is required.

Incremental backup

Incremental backup backs up only the changed data since the last backup, whether it is a full or incremental backup. Suppose you had taken full backup on Sunday. On Monday, you will take incremental backup of changed files since Sunday. On Tuesday if you take incremental backup once again, it will backup only files that has changed since last incremental backup i.e. since Monday. However, if you take differential backup on Tuesday it will take backup of all files that have changed since full backup i.e. Sunday. To restore incremental backup, you require full backup and all incremental backups since last full backup.

Backup tools for RHEL

RHEL provides some basic tools to take backup. If you require advanced features, you can use proprietary tools which provides automated backup, backup over network, backup using own database etc.

RHEL basic tools for full and partial backup are following

- Tar
- CPIO
- dump and restore

Advanced utility for RHEL backup

The Advanced Maryland Automatic Network Disk Archiver (AMANDA) client/ server based utility which uses dump or tar to take backup over network.

Proprietary tools for backup

Some of the corporate tools for backup which are more advanced and feature rich :-

- IBM's Tivoli Storage Manager
- Veritas Netbackup
- EMC NetWorker
- HPE StoreOnce

RHEL backup tools explained

Tar

Tar is the most versatile tool in Unix and Linux to take backup. Tar command can be used to create one archive file of multiple files. You can copy tar archive files to tape, DVD or USB drive as a backup. You can also create compressed file by adding options while creating achieve file.

Create tar

Syntax

```
tar cvf name_of_archive_file files_or_directory_to_archive
```

Where

c   create

v   verbose

f   file name types of achieve file

Example

```
# cd /var/log
# tar cvf /backup/varlogs.tar *.log
boot.log
vmware-vmsvc.log
vmware-vmusr.log
wpa_supplicant.log
Xorg.0.log
Xorg.1.log
Xorg.9.log
yum.log
# ls -la /backup
total 144
drwxr-xr-x.  2 root root       25 Mar  8 04:11 .
dr-xr-xr-x. 21 root root     4096 Mar  8 04:07 ..
-rw-r--r--.  1 root root 143360 Mar  8 04:11 varlogs.tar
```

Create compressed tar file

You can compress the archive backup using tar options. Tar provides two type of compression gzip and bzip.

Create gzip format tar file

Syntax

```
# tar cvfz nameoftarfile.tar.gz name_of_files
```

125

Example

```
# tar cvfz /backup/varlogs.tar.gz *.log
```

Create bzip format

Syntax

```
# tar cvfj nameoftarfile.tar.bz2 name_of_files
```

Example

```
# tar cvfj /backup/varlogs.tar.bz2 *.log
```

Extract

To restore the files taken backup with tar command

```
# tar xvf /backup/varlogs.tar
```

Where

x   extract

v   verbose

f   file name types of achieve file

gzip format

Syntax

```
tar xvfz filename
```

Example

```
# tar xvfz /backup/varlogs.tar.gz
```

bzip format

Syntax

```
tar xvfj filename
```

Example

```
# tar xvfj /backup/varlogs.tar.bz2
```

List

Use **t** option to show content of archive file. Same command can be used to list the content of compressed files

List the archived tar file

Syntax

```
tar tvf filename
```

Example

```
# tar tvf /backup/varlogs.tar
# tar tvf /backup/varlogs.tar.bz2
# tar tvf /backup/varlogs.tar.gz
```

CPIO

CPIO utility copies files from and to achieve. It can be used to achieve and to copy files from one place to another.

To archive all files in **/var/log** folder to **backup** folder

```
# cd /var/log
# ls |cpio -ov > /backup/varlogs.cpio
```

To extract files from CPIO backup

```
# mkdir newbackup
# cd newbackup
# cpio -idv < /backup/varlogs.cpio
```

Creating archive from list of specific files.

Example :- archive all files with log extension from **var** directory

```
# find /var -iname *.log -print|cpio -ov > /backup/varlog.cpio
```

CPIO to create tar file

```
# ls|cpio -ovH tar -F abc.tar
```

To extract tar file using CPIO

```
# cpio -idv -F abc.tar
```

dump and restore

xfsdump

xfsdump utility is used to take backup of whole file system or files that has changed since last dump. Ideally, dump should be taken on the quiescent file system, so that files should not change during backup.

Syntax

```
xfsdump <options> target_device  filessystem_tobe backed_up
```

Example

To take backup of whole root filesystem to device st0

```
# xfsdump -l 0 -f /dev/st0 /
```

Where

-l   for dumpl level . There are ten dump levels from **0 to 9**

    0   complete

    1   increment from last backup

2-9 increment from last incremental backup

-f for device name

xfsrestore

xfsrestore command is used to restore the backup taken with dump command

Syntax

```
xfsrestore <options> backupdevice target
```

Example

To restore backup stored on /dev/st0 device

```
# xfsrestore –f /dev/st0 /home1
```

where option

-f is for device name

Chapter 15.

Archiving and Compression

Archiving is the process of collecting and storing a group of files and directories into one file, Tar, cpio, zip and ar are example of utilities which performs this action. Whereas compression is processes of reducing the size of files using mathematical compression algorithm. It is quite useful in sending large files over the internet. Example of compression utilities are gzip, bzip2, xz etc.

GZIP

With gzip you can compress and decompress individual file. When you give gzip command to compress any file, the file will be replaced with extension .gz file keeping the same ownership modes, access and modification times. In sort, you will not see original file only compressed file will be there.

Syntax

```
gzip filename
```

Example

```
gzip sysctl.conf
```

Decompress

To decompress the compressed file use **gunzip** command. However this command will remove the compressed file you will see only uncompressed file only.

130

Syntax

```
gunzip filename
```

Example

```
gunzip sysctl.conf.gz
```

BZIP2

Bzip compresses file using compression algorithm known as Burrows Wheel block sorting. Like gzip it removes the original file and creates compressed file with same name plus extension bz2. Each compressed file has same modification date, permission and if possible with same ownership as corresponding original file.

Syntax

```
bzip2 filename
```

Example

```
bzip2 sysctl.conf
```

Decompress

To decompress the file compressed with bzip2 command use bunzip2. By default it will not overwrite if file of same name exist unless you give –f option

Syntax

```
bunzip2 filename
```

Example

```
bunzip2 sysctl.conf.bz2
```

XZ

xz is successor of the lzma utility, it will add .xz extension to compressed file automatically and remove original file. Like bzip and gzip it will keep same modification date, permission and if possible with same ownership as corresponding original file.

Syntax

```
xz filename
```

Example

```
xz sysctl.conf
```

Decompress

Syntax

```
unxz filename
```

Example

```
unxz sysctl.conf.xz
```

ZIP

Zip is archiving and compression utility. It creates files with .zip extension. It is cross platform compression utility so you can compress and decompress files from Linux to windows or vice versa. It will keep the original files intact

Syntax

```
zip zipfile.zip file/files_to_compress
```

Example

```
zip abc.zip sysctl.conf signond.conf
```

you can use zip also with wild cards

```
zip abc.zip s*
```

Zip files recursively (include sub directories also)

Syntax
```
zip -r zipfile.zip directoryname
```

Example
```
zip -r asp.zip monk
```

Listing content of compressed file

Syntax
```
unzip -l zipfile.zip
```

Example
```
unzip -l asp.zip
```

Decompress

To decompress compressed files with zip command unzip is used

Syntax
```
unzip zipfile.zip
```

Example
```
unzip asp.zip
```

ar

ar is not so known predecessor of rar which is in still in use in RHEL. It used for archiving only as such there is no compression in it.

Create archive

Syntax

```
ar cvsr archivefile.a files_to_archive
```

Example

```
ar cvsr abc.a s*
```

Extract archive

Syntax

```
ar xv archivefile.a
```

Example

```
ar xv abc.a
```

There are many third party utilities available which can be installed, you can try following

- peazip
- p7zip
- pax
- kgb

Many more..

## Chapter 16

Firewall

According to dictionary, a firewall is a wall or partition designed to inhibit or prevent the spread of fire. In computer world, firewall is network security system used to secure the incoming and outgoing connections. It prevents unauthorized access to the system. It restricts user to access only designated services.

nftables

In earlier version of Redhat iptables were used for packet filtering, but in with Redhat 8 it has been replaced with nftables. it is single tool for all iptable framework like iptables, ip6tables, arptables etc. It allows you to perform packet filtering (firewalling), NAT, mangling and packet classification. Now you can build firewall over nftables. nftables by default does not pre-create tables and chains like its predecessor, iptables, which results in increase in system performance.

Check if system is using nftables

```
# iptables --version
iptables v1.8.2 (nf_tables)
```

Firewalld

Firewalld is the dynamic firewall manager. Changes can be done immediately in the runtime environment. No restart of the service is needed. firewalld use nft binary to interacts with nftables. It is an interface and connects to the netfilter kernel code. FirewallD uses services and zones. firewalld stores its rules in various XML files under

/usr/lib/firewalld/ and **/etc/firewalld/** folders. Firewalld allows security configuration without stopping current configuration. In earlier version with **iptables** every change requires flushing of all old rules and reading new rules from iptable configuration file, but in firewalld only new differences are applied without disturbing current connections.

A command-line client **firewall-cmd**, is provided. It can be used to make permanent and runtime changes to firewall rules. You require to be root or with administrative privileges to run **firewalld-cmd** command

Install firewalld

```
# yum install firewalld
```

Check the status

```
# systemctl status firewalld
```
or

```
# firewall-cmd --state
running
```

Firewalld concepts

Configuration options

Rules of firewalld can be designated as either Permanent or Runtime. Runtime changes are those changes to firewall settings that take effect immediately but are not permanently. Runtime changes will not retain after reboot of system or configuration reload. Whereas permanent changes are those changes which are written into configuration files but will not be applied immediately unless you reload the configuration or reboot the machine.

Zones

In firewalld concept of zone is based on network interface. All network interfaces can be located in the same default zone or divided into different zones according to the levels of trust defined. By defualt public zone is used for configuration. If you have more than one interface than you can create more zones and restrict trafic between zones. Lets take example if we have web server having two interface one connecting to outside world i.e. public zone and second interface in trusted zone that connects to database server.

Note: Without any configuration, everything is done by default in the public zone.

List of zones with explanation

- **Drop**

  Drop all incoming connections, only outgoing network connections are available.

- **Block**

  Allows only outgoing network connection. Reject all incoming connection with icmp-host-prohibited message.

- **Public**

  You do not trust the other computers on the network. Only selected incoming connections are accepted. For use in public areas.

- **Home**

  Only selected incoming connections are accepted. For use in home area

- **Work**

  You mostly trust the other computers on networks. Only selected incoming connections are accepted. For use in work areas.

- **DMZ**

  For the computers in DMZ demilitarized zone that are publicly accessible with limited access to the internal network, only selected incoming connections are accepted.

- **External**

  For use on external networks with masquerading enabled. Only selected incoming connections are accepted.

- **Internal**

  For use on internal networks. You mostly trust the other computers on the networks. Only selected incoming connections are accepted.

- **Trusted**

  All network connections are accepted.

Zones commands

List the available zones

```
# firewall-cmd --get-zones
```

To display default zone

```
# firewall-cmd --get-default-zone
```

Change the default zone

```
# firewall-cmd --set-default-zone= internal
```

Check the zone to which interface is associated with

```
# firewall-cmd --get-zone-of-interface=ens33
```

Where ens33 is interface name you can check this using ip add show command

Change the zone of the interface

```
# firewall-cmd --permanent --zone=internal --change-interface= ens33
```

Services

Firewalld services allows network traffic based on predefined rules. A Firewalld service can be a list of local ports, protocols and destinations. You can also create your own custom rules for services. The **/usr/lib/firewalld/services** directory contains configuration files for default supported services and custom service files created by users are located in **/etc/firewalld/services** directory.

List of services in the default zone

```
# firewall-cmd --list-services
```

Add a service permanently to default zone

Syntax

```
# firewall-cmd --permanent --add-service=servicename
```

Example

```
# firewall-cmd --permanent --add-service=http
```

After that, you have to reload the new configuration

```
# firewall-cmd --reload
```

Add service to specific zone

```
# firewall-cmd --permanent --zone=internal --add-service=http
```

Port

Firewalld allows us to manage the network port directly.

List of ports in the default zone

```
# firewall-cmd --list-ports
```

Opening Port in the Firewall

To open up a new port (e.g., TCP/5903) permanently, use these commands.

```
# firewall-cmd --permanent --zone=public --add-port=5903/tcp
```

Then reload the configuration

```
# firewall-cmd --reload
```

Check the new configuration

```
# firewall-cmd --list-ports
```

Firewall configuration using GUI

If you do not like to use commands, Redhat also provides GUI interface for configuration of firewall.

Installation

If GUI firewall is not already installed it can be installed with following command

```
# yum install firewall-config
```

There are two version of firewall interface, the first one is a version that runs under Gnome, and second one works on the command line. Here we will discuss Gnome version.

To start the GUI login as root on Gnome terminal

Run terminal window

In the terminal windows write following command

```
# firewall-config
```

It will open firewall interface

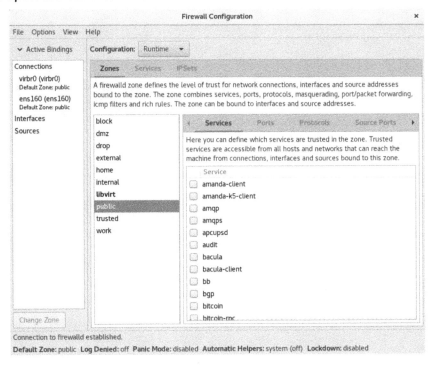

Changing the Firewall Settings

Changing Configuration

When you start the interface, **Runtime** configuration is selected from the configuration dropdown menu for immediate change in the current firewall settings, Alternatively to apply the setting on next system start or firewall configuration reload , select Permanent from the drop-down list.

Change zone of Connection

To configure or add connection to a zone start firewall-config , from the option menu select **Change zone of connections**. It will show sub menu with list of connections available, select the desired connection from the dropdown menu. From next dropdown menu, select the Zone.

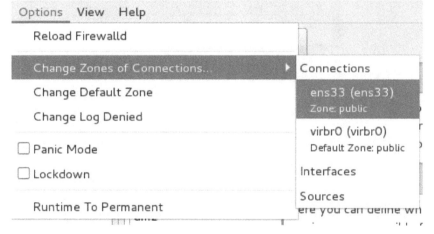

Set default zone

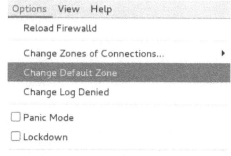

To set the default zone for new interface or change the default zone for a existing interface, start **firewall-config**, First select the desired connection then select Options from the menu bar, and select **Change Default Zone** from the drop-down menu. Now select the require zone from the list Menu.

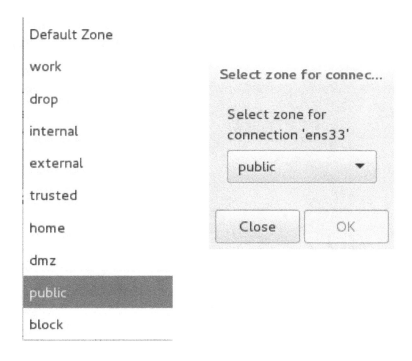

Configuring services

Firewall-config tool provides interface to enable and disable predefined or custom services.

1. select the configuration type permanent or runtime
2. Select zone.
3. Select or deselect the service check box. Selected check box means service is enabled and cleared (un-selected) checkbox is to block the service.

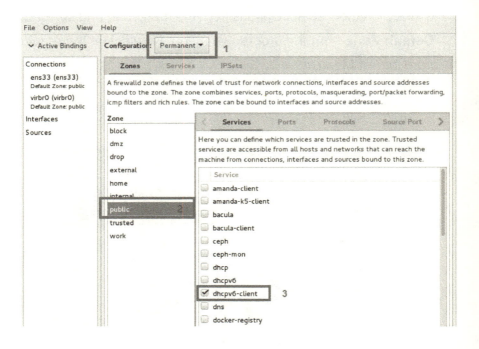

## Chapter 17

Partition

Hard disk or hard drive is piece of hardware installed in your PC or server that stores data and provides quick access to large amounts of data on an electromagnetically charged surface or set of chips. Today capacity of hard disk can be in gigabytes and terabytes of storage. Hard disk can be attached internally or externally. With ever increasing capacity of hard disk you are tempted to install more than one Operating system on the same machine, for that you do partitioning of hard disk. Partitioning is also useful in keeping Operating system, application and data separate for better storage management.

Partitions

Partition in computer language is to divide the storage, mostly hard disk into segments in which you can have more than one file systems. Partitioning of storage helps in better storage management and easy backup. There are variety of tools available in Linux for storage partitioning like fdisk, Gnome disks and Parted etc. We will discuss two main tools fdisk and parted in this chapter.

Fdisk

fdisk is a powerful and most popular command line tool used for partition management. It is a text based menu-driven program for creation and manipulation of partition tables. It supports multiple types of partition tables formats, including MS-DOS and GPT. It provides interface to display, create, resize, delete and modify partitions on disks.

Fdisk for partition management

List the partition table

```
fdisk -l
```

List the partition table for specific

Syntax

```
fdisk -l <device name >
```

Example

```
fdisk -l /dev/hda1
```

Create new partition on device

In this example /dev/sdb is added to system

1. First print the list of all storage devices and check the device name for the device on which you want to create partition

```
# fdisk -l
Disk /dev/sdb: 21.5 GB, 21474836480 bytes
255 heads, 63 sectors/track, 2610 cylinders
Units = cylinders of 16065 * 512 = 8225280 bytes
Sector size (logical/physical): 512 bytes / 512 bytes
----Output is truncated -----
```

It will show the all storage device

2. Run fdisk on required device

```
# fdisk -cu /dev/sdb
```

146

3. Print the partition table of selected device

Press **p** and **enter** key

```
Command (m for help): p

Disk /dev/sdb: 21.5 GB, 21474836480 bytes
255 heads, 63 sectors/track, 2610 cylinders, total 41943040
sectors
Units = sectors of 1 * 512 = 512 bytes
Sector size (logical/physical): 512 bytes / 512 bytes
I/O size (minimum/optimal): 512 bytes / 512 bytes
Disk identifier: 0xdec2ee90


   Device Boot        Start          End      Blocks   Id  System
```

Output shows no partition present on sdb device

4. Press **n** to create new partition

```
Command (m for help): n
```

5. Press **p** to set partition type as primary or Press **e** for extended
   partition

```
Command action
   e   extended
   p   primary partition (1-4)
p
```

6. Give partition number like **1, 2, 3, 4.** If it is first partition on this
   device then press 1 for second partition press 2 like that

```
Partition number (1-4): 1
```

7. Press enter to use default starting sector or you can enter desired value if you do not want to start from the default sector

```
First sector (2048-41943039, default 2048):
Using default value 2048
```

8. For last sector, if you can calculate the size with sector numbers you can give sector number, otherwise you can give size in human readable value like +1G to create 1 GB partition. If you press **Enter** without any value it will create partition on whole remaining space on the device

```
Last sector, +sectors or +size{K,M,G} (2048-41943039, default
41943039): +1G
```

9. Press **w** to write on disk

Delete the partition

To delete partition present on disk drive using fdisk following procedure is there. In this example device name is /dev/sdb and we want to delete the /dev/sdb2 partition.

Display partition table of the desired device

```
[root@RHEL2 ~]# fdisk -l /dev/sdb

Disk /dev/sdb: 21.5 GB, 21474836480 bytes, 41943040 sectors
Units = sectors of 1 * 512 = 512 bytes
Sector size (logical/physical): 512 bytes / 512 bytes
I/O size (minimum/optimal): 512 bytes / 512 bytes
Disk label type: dos
Disk identifier: 0xd397c54b
```

```
Device Boot        Start        End        Blocks   Id  System
/dev/sdb1           2048     1955839        976896   83  Linux
/dev/sdb2        1955840    41943039      19993600   83  Linux
```

Once you know the device partition number to delete give disk command with device name

```
[root@RHEL2 ~]# fdisk /dev/sdb
Welcome to fdisk (util-linux 2.23.2).

Changes will remain in memory only, until you decide to write
them.
Be careful before using the write command.

Command (m for help):
```

Press 'd' to delete the partition

```
Command (m for help): d
```

Give the partition number to delete in this case partition number is 2 . press 2 and press **Enter**.

```
Partition number (1,2, default 2): 2
Partition 2 is deleted
```

Print the new partition table by pressing p and **Enter**

```
Command (m for help): p

Disk /dev/sdb: 21.5 GB, 21474836480 bytes, 41943040 sectors
Units = sectors of 1 * 512 = 512 bytes
Sector size (logical/physical): 512 bytes / 512 bytes
I/O size (minimum/optimal): 512 bytes / 512 bytes
```

```
Disk label type: dos
Disk identifier: 0xd397c54b


   Device Boot        Start          End      Blocks   Id  System
/dev/sdb1                2048      1955839      976896   83  Linux
```

Write the changes by pressing **w** key. You will lose all changes if you
quite without writing, as all these changes are still in memory.

```
Command (m for help): w
The partition table has been altered!
Calling ioctl() to re-read partition table.
Syncing disks.
```

Alter partition

You can use fdisk to alter partition also . In this example we will change
the partition type from Linux to Linux LVM

1. First view the current partition table of selected device.
2. Run the **fdisk** with selected device.
3. Select the partition by pressing the partition number.
4. Press **t** to change partition type.
5. Now list the partition types and their Hex code by pressing **L**.
6. Provide the required hex code in this example it is **8e.**
7. Press **w** to write the changes.

```
[root@RHEL2 ~]# fdisk -l /dev/sdb

Disk /dev/sdb: 21.5 GB, 21474836480 bytes, 41943040 sectors
Units = sectors of 1 * 512 = 512 bytes
Sector size (logical/physical): 512 bytes / 512 bytes
I/O size (minimum/optimal): 512 bytes / 512 bytes
Disk label type: dos
```

```
Disk identifier: 0xd397c54b

Device Boot      Start        End      Blocks   Id  System
/dev/sdb1         2048    2099199     1048576   83  Linux
/dev/sdb2      2099200   41943039    19921920   83  Linux
```

Now run fdisk with device name

```
[root@RHEL2 ~]# fdisk /dev/sdb
Welcome to fdisk (util-linux 2.23.2).

Changes will remain in memory only, until you decide to write
them.
Be careful before using the write command.
To change partition type
Command (m for help): t
Partition number (1,2, default 2): 1
Hex code (type L to list all codes): L


0   Empty          24  NEC DOS          81  Minix / old Lin bf  Solaris
1   FAT12          27  Hidden NTFS Win  82  Linux swap / So  c1  DRDOS/sec
(FAT-
2   XENIX root     39  Plan 9           83  Linux            c4  DRDOS/sec
(FAT-
3   XENIX usr      3c  PartitionMagic   84  OS/2 hidden C:   c6  DRDOS/sec
(FAT-
4   FAT16 <32M     40  Venix 80286      85  Linux extended   c7  Syrinx
5   Extended       41  PPC PReP Boot    86  NTFS volume set  da  Non-FS data
6   FAT16          42  SFS              87  NTFS volume set  db  CP/M / CTOS /
.
7   HPFS/NTFS/exFAT 4d  QNX4.x          88  Linux plaintext  de  Dell Utility
8   AIX            4e  QNX4.x 2nd part 8e  Linux LVM        df  BootIt
9   AIX bootable   4f  QNX4.x 3rd part 93  Amoeba           e1  DOS access
a   OS/2 Boot Manag 50  OnTrack DM      94  Amoeba BBT       e3  DOS R/O
b   W95 FAT32      51  OnTrack DM6 Aux 9f  BSD/OS           e4  SpeedStor
```

151

```
  c   W95 FAT32 (LBA) 52   CP/M              a0   IBM Thinkpad hi eb   BeOS fs

  e   W95 FAT16 (LBA) 53   OnTrack DM6 Aux a5   FreeBSD              ee   GPT

  f   W95 Ext'd (LBA) 54   OnTrackDM6      a6   OpenBSD              ef   EFI (FAT-

12/16/

 10   OPUS            55   EZ-Drive        a7   NeXTSTEP             f0   Linux/PA-RISC

 b

 11   Hidden FAT12    56   Golden Bow      a8   Darwin UFS           f1   SpeedStor

 12   Compaq diagnost 5c   Priam Edisk     a9   NetBSD               f4   SpeedStor

 14   Hidden FAT16 <3 61   SpeedStor       ab   Darwin boot          f2   DOS secondary

 16   Hidden FAT16    63   GNU HURD or Sys af   HFS / HFS+           fb   VMware VMFS

 17   Hidden HPFS/NTF 64   Novell Netware  b7   BSDI fs              fc   VMware

VMKCORE

 18   AST SmartSleep  65   Novell Netware  b8   BSDI swap            fd   Linux raid

auto

 1b   Hidden W95 FAT3 70   DiskSecure Mult bb   Boot Wizard hid fe   LANstep

 1c   Hidden W95 FAT3 75   PC/IX           be   Solaris boot         ff   BBT

 1e   Hidden W95 FAT1 80   Old Minix

Hex code (type L to list all codes): 8e

Changed type of partition 'Linux' to 'Linux LVM'


Command (m for help): w

The partition table has been altered!


Calling ioctl() to re-read partition table.

Syncing disks.
```

Now list the partition to verify

```
[root@RHEL2 ~]# fdisk -l /dev/sdb


Disk /dev/sdb: 21.5 GB, 21474836480 bytes, 41943040 sectors

Units = sectors of 1 * 512 = 512 bytes

Sector size (logical/physical): 512 bytes / 512 bytes

I/O size (minimum/optimal): 512 bytes / 512 bytes

Disk label type: dos
```

```
Disk identifier: 0xd397c54b

Device Boot      Start        End       Blocks   Id  System
/dev/sdb1         2048    2099199      1048576   8e  Linux LVM
/dev/sdb2      2099200   41943039     19921920   83  Linux
```

Parted

Parted is an other famous command line tool that allows you to easily manage hard disk partitions. The utility parted allows users to:

- View the existing partition table
- Add partitions from free space
- Delete existing partitions

Install Parted on Linux

If parted is not installed on your Linux machine you can install it using following command

```
# yum install parted
```

Check version of installed parted

To know version of installed parted either you can give parted -v

```
[root@RHEL2 ~]# parted -v
parted (GNU parted) 3.2
Copyright (C) 2014 Free Software Foundation, Inc.
License GPLv3+: GNU GPL version 3 or later
<http://gnu.org/licenses/gpl.html>.
This is free software: you are free to change and redistribute
it.
There is NO WARRANTY, to the extent permitted by law..
```

List partitions

To list partition start parted and give `print` command or

parted -l

```
[root@RHEL2 ~]# parted -l
Model: VMware, VMware Virtual S (scsi)
Disk /dev/sda: 21.5GB
Sector size (logical/physical): 512B/512B
Partition Table: msdos
Disk Flags:

Number  Start   End     Size    Type     File system     Flags
 1      1049kB  10.7GB  10.7GB  primary  xfs             boot
 2      10.7GB  15.0GB  4295MB  primary  linux-swap(v1)

<output truncated >
```

List Partition of specific disk

To list partition of specific disk, give parted command with device name then use `print` and quit command.

```
[root@RHEL2 ~]# parted /dev/sda
GNU Parted 3.1
Using /dev/sda
Welcome to GNU Parted! Type 'help' to view a list of commands.
(parted) print
Model: VMware, VMware Virtual S (scsi)
Disk /dev/sda: 21.5GB
Sector size (logical/physical): 512B/512B
Partition Table: msdos
Disk Flags:
```

154

```
Number  Start   End     Size    Type     File system     Flags
1       1049kB  10.7GB  10.7GB  primary  xfs             boot
2       10.7GB  15.0GB  4295MB  primary  linux-swap(v1)
(parted) quit
```

Create partition

Define partition type

First thing when add new disk you have to decide partition style it can be either MBR or GPT.

MBR and GPT are two style of partitioning. Master boot record (MBR) is old standard supported by most of the OS. MBR disk use the standard BIOS partition table. On the other hand, GUID partition table (GPT) is a new technology in which disks uses unified extensible firmware interface (UEFI). The advantage of GPT disks is that you can have more than four partitions on each disk and it can support disks larger than 2 terabytes.

To change the partition type with parted command, use **mklabel** command option followed by partition type, Use mklabel **msdos** command for MBR type partition write mklabel **gpt** for GPT type partition.

```
[root@RHEL2 ~]# parted /dev/sdb
GNU Parted 3.1
Using /dev/sdb
Welcome to GNU Parted! Type 'help' to view a list of commands.
(parted) mklabel msdos
Warning: The existing disk label on /dev/sdb will be destroyed
and all data on this disk will be lost. Do you want to
continue?
```

```
Yes/No? yes
(parted)
```

Create partition

Once defined the partition style it's time to create partition.

Following are the steps to create partition

1. Give **parted** command with required device name
2. use **mkpart** command
3. Select partition type, it can be primary **or extended**
4. Give file system type default is **ext2**
5. Like fdisk give starting and ending sector number if disk is new starting sector will be 1 and for ending you can give size like 1G for 1GB partition size

```
(parted) mkpart
Partition type?  primary/extended? primary
File system type?  [ext2]?
Start? 1
End? 1G
(parted) print
Model: VMware, VMware Virtual S (scsi)
Disk /dev/sdb: 21.5GB
Sector size (logical/physical): 512B/512B
Partition Table: msdos
Disk Flags:

Number  Start    End      Size    Type      File system  Flags
 1       1049kB  1000MB   999MB   primary
(parted) quite
```

Add partition

If you have space available on the hard disk and you want to add one more partition you can give **mkpart** command in parted interface. It will ask same question as in case of creating first partition. However, this time start will be end of the previous partition as start of this partition plus size of the partition is the **end** of the partition. In this example, start is 1000MB as the end is at 1000MB for first partition and end of this partition will be 2000MB(1000MB + 1000MB) if you want add 1000MB partition.

```
(parted) mkpart
Partition type?  primary/extended? primary
File system type?  [ext2]?
Start? 1000MB
End? 2000MB
(parted) print
Model: VMware, VMware Virtual S (scsi)
Disk /dev/sdb: 21.5GB
Sector size (logical/physical): 512B/512B
Partition Table: msdos
Disk Flags:

Number  Start    End     Size   Type      File system  Flags
  1       1049kB  1000MB  999MB  primary
  2       1000MB  2000MB  999MB  primary
```

Delete partition

To delete the partition use `rm partition_number` command.

Example

```
(parted) print
Model: VMware, VMware Virtual S (scsi)
Disk /dev/sdb: 21.5GB
```

157

```
Sector size (logical/physical): 512B/512B
Partition Table: msdos
Disk Flags:

Number  Start   End     Size    Type      File system  Flags
 1       1049kB  1000MB  999MB   primary
 2       1001MB  2001MB  999MB   primary
 3       2001MB  3001MB  1000MB  primary


(parted) rm 3
(parted) print
Model: VMware, VMware Virtual S (scsi)
Disk /dev/sdb: 21.5GB
Sector size (logical/physical): 512B/512B
Partition Table: msdos
Disk Flags:

Number  Start   End     Size    Type     File system  Flags
 1       1049kB  1000MB  999MB   primary
 2       1001MB  2001MB  999MB   primary
```

In this Chapter, we learned how to manage partitions, in the next chapter we will discuss how to create file system on these partitions.

## Chapter 18

File system

File System is method used by operating system to store and retrieve data. File system helps in managing and arranging data. There are different types of file systems available in Linux. Each type of file system uses different structure and logic for storing and retrieving data. Some file systems have been specifically designed for specific devices and applications, for example ISO 9660 file system is used for optical disks like CDROM. Depending of file system type it can be local or over network. Linux support wide variety of file systems each file system has pros and cons. We will discuss some of the common filesystems used in RHEL. In RHEL 8 BTRFS file system has been removed. This means you will not be able to create, mount or install Btrfs file system on RHEL 8 machine.

XFS

XFS is a high-performance journaling file system that was initially created by Silicon Graphics, Inc. for the IRIX operating system and later ported to Linux. XFS supports metadata journaling, which facilitates quicker crash recovery. The XFS file system can also be defragmented and enlarged while mounted and active. XFS records file system updates asynchronously to a circular buffer (the journal) before it can commit the actual data updates to disk. XFS is default File system for RHEL 8. New features copy-on-write data extents has been added to XFS. This feature allows two or more files to share a common set of data blocks. When there is change on either of the files sharing common blocks, XFS breaks the link to common blocks and creates a new file. This helps in saving space and disk writes.

Creating XFS file system

1. Create partition using fdisk as described in the earlier chapter
2. **fdisk -l check** the required device name
3. **mkfs -t xfs /dev/sdb1** where **sdb1** is device name and **xfs is** file system type.

```
~]# mkfs -t xfs /dev/sdb1
```

4. **create mount point**

```
~]# mkdir /test1
```

5. **Add entry in the /etc/fstab**

```
~]# vi /etc/fstab
/dev/mapper/cl-root /      xfs      defaults        1 1
UUID=6b761a5f-8c7c-465d-b58c-d29267938403 /boot  xfs defaults        1 2
/dev/mapper/cl-swap swap swap     defaults        0 0
/dev/sdb1          /test1          xfs      defaults        0 2
```

Where **/dev/sdb1** is device **/test1** mount point, **xfs** for partition type, 0 for dump and 2 order for fsck.

EXT File System

Extended file system (EXT) is most popular file system used in Linux Operating systems. In its lifespan it had evolved a lot from its first implementation in 1992 to till date. EXT 4 is the most recent version of EXT. From third generation i.e. **EXT 3** it came up with journalized file system. With JFS feature it keep the track of changes not yet committed to the file system by recording such changes in data structure to journal which in turn generate circular log. In case of abrupt system down like

160

power failure, crashed file system can be brought back online easily. **EXT3** having limitation of file system size as 8TB /16TB and file size as 2 TB whereas **Ext4** is the next generation of ext file system having improved file system and file size upper limits of 16TB. It is efficient reliable and robust. In RHEL 8 ext4 metadata is protected by checksums. This enables the file system to identify the corrupt metadata, this results increase in the file system resilience.

Creating EXT4 file system

1. Create partition with fdisk
2. **fdisk -l** check the device name
3. **mkfs -t ext4 /dev/sdb1** where **sdb1** is device name and **ext4** is file system type

Syntax

```
mkfs -t ext4 device_name
```

Example

```
~]# mkfs -t ext4 /dev/sdb1
```

Or

```
~]# mkfs.ext4 /dev/sdb1
```

4. **create mount point**

```
~]# mkdir /test1
```

5. **Mount new File system**

```
~]# mount -t ext4 /dev/sdb1 /test1
```

6. Add entry in the /etc/fstab

```
~]# vi /etc/fstab
/dev/mapper/cl-root /    xfs      defaults        1 1
UUID=6b761a5f-8c7c-465d-b58c-d29267938403 /boot  xfs defaults        1 2
/dev/mapper/cl-swap swap swap     defaults        0 0
/dev/sdb1       /test1          ext4      defaults        0 2
```

## Chapter 19

Swap space

Swap space is used in Linux and UNIX to free up physical memory. The inactive pages of data are written to slower storage i.e. hard disk. The area where inactive data is written is called as swap space.

Add swap space

1. Create partition

```
~]# fdisk /dev/sdb

WARNING: DOS-compatible mode is deprecated. It's strongly
recommended to switch off the mode (command 'c') and change
display units to sectors (command 'u').

Command (m for help): n
Command action
   e    extended
   p    primary partition (1-4)
p
Partition number (1-4): 2
First cylinder (307-6132, default 307):
Using default value 307
Last cylinder, +cylinders or +size{K,M,G} (307-6132, default
6132): +1G
```

Change the type by pressing **t** of partition selected to **82** which is Linux swap

```
Command (m for help): t
Partition number (1-4): 2
Hex code (type L to list codes): 82
Changed system type of partition 2 to 82 (Linux swap /
Solaris)

Check the partition
Command (m for help): p

Disk /dev/sdb: 21.5 GB, 21474836480 bytes
171 heads, 40 sectors/track, 6132 cylinders
Units = cylinders of 6840 * 512 = 3502080 bytes
Sector size (logical/physical): 512 bytes / 512 bytes
I/O size (minimum/optimal): 512 bytes / 512 bytes
Disk identifier: 0xdec2ee90

Device Boot    Start    End      Blocks    Id  System
/dev/sdb1        1      307     1048576    83  Linux
/dev/sdb2       307     614     1050280    82  Linux swap /
Solaris

Press w to write partition to disk
Command (m for help): w
The partition table has been altered!

Calling ioctl() to re-read partition table.
Syncing disks.
```

2. **mkswap /dev/sdb2** where sdb2 is name of the partition which will
   be used as swap.

```
~]# mkswap /dev/sdb2
Setting up swapspace version 1, size = 1050276 KiB
no label, UUID=c1f98067-9548-4bf1-843d-5f09f5d5ba56
```

3. Add entry in /etc/fstab

```
~]# cat /etc/fstab

/dev/mapper/cl-root /    xfs     defaults        1 1
UUID=6b761a5f-8c7c-465d-b58c-d29267938403 boot xfs
defaults        1 2
/dev/mapper/cl-swap swap                    swap    defaults
0 0
/dev/sdb1       /test1          xfs     defaults        0 2
UUID=c1f98067-9548-..5ba56 swap swap    defaults        0 0
```

4. swapon -a will activate swap

5. swapon -s will show status of all swap space

```
~]# swapon -s
Filename              Type          Size     Used
Priority
/dev/dm-1             partition     2097144 0        -1
/dev/sdb2            partition     1050272 0        -2
```

To deactivate the swap space

```
# swapoff /dev/sdb2
```

Chapter 20.

Logical Volume Manager

In earlier section we have learned about creating Linux partition but Linux provides option to create partition type as LVM (logical partition manager). LVM is more sophisticated than normal Linux partition. LVM offers following benefits

- Increase the File system dynamically
- Shrink the File system
- Add disk dynamically
- Mirroring
- Stripping
- Snapshot as backup of File system

Terms used in LVM

Physical Volume

Physical Volume (PV) is physical storage unit of an LVM is a block device such as a partition or whole disk. To use the device for an LVM create partition with **fdisk** as **LVM** type.

Volume Groups

One or more physical volumes combined into Volume Group (VG). Volume group is an abstract that presents underlying devices as a unified logical device with combined storage capacity of the physical volumes

Physical Extent

Storage space from Physical Volume is divided in to small unit of fixed size known as physical extent, which is smallest unit that can be allocated. P.E. size is always same for all physical volume in the same VG.

Logical extent

Mapping of PE to make up frontend of LVM. By default, one PE is generally mapped to one LE. However, you can map more than one PE to one LE in case of mirroring.

Logical Volume

Logical volume is group of Logical Extent. It is here we create File system. Logical volume is not restricted to physical disk sizes. In additionto that, the hardware storage layer is isolated from software.

Steps to create File system on new disk added to the system

1. Create Physical volume (PV)

Scan the new disk

If you plugged the hot swap disk or added the virtual disk to virtual machine while machine is running, to detect the new disk on the SCSI bus use following script. This script is to avoid server restart, if you can reboot the machine this step is not required as during boot process system will automatically add the newly installed disk.

167

```
for host in `ls /sys/class/scsi_host/`;do
echo "- - -" >/sys/class/scsi_host/${host}/scan;
done
```

Change disk partition as LVM

Use **fdisk** command and create partition type Linux LVM **8e.** This step can be ignored if whole disk is used as PV.

```
~]# fdisk /dev/sdb


WARNING: DOS-compatible mode is deprecated. It's strongly
recommended to
        switch off the mode (command 'c') and change display
units to
        sectors (command 'u').
Command (m for help): n
Command action
   e   extended
   p   primary partition (1-4)
p
Partition number (1-4): 3
First cylinder (615-6132, default 615):
Using default value 615
Last cylinder, +cylinders or +size{K,M,G} (615-6132, default
6132): +5G

Command (m for help): t
Partition number (1-4): 3
Hex code (type L to list codes): 8e
Changed system type of partition 3 to 8e (Linux LVM)

Command (m for help): p
```

168

```
Disk /dev/sdb: 21.5 GB, 21474836480 bytes
171 heads, 40 sectors/track, 6132 cylinders
Units = cylinders of 6840 * 512 = 3502080 bytes
Sector size (logical/physical): 512 bytes / 512 bytes
I/O size (minimum/optimal): 512 bytes / 512 bytes
Disk identifier: 0xdec2ee90


Device Boot       Start        End       Blocks   Id  System
/dev/sdb1             1        307      1048576   83  Linux
/dev/sdb2           307        614      1050280   82  Linux swap
/ Solaris
/dev/sdb3           615       2148      5246280   8e  Linux LVM


Command (m for help): w
The partition table has been altered!
```

Use pvcreate commad

Create PV using command **pvcreate** *device_name* where *device_name* is device created with fdisk. If it is whole disk, use the device name

```
~]# pvcreate /dev/sdb3
    Physical volume "/dev/sdb3" successfully created
~]# pvdisplay /dev/sdb3
    "/dev/sdb3" is a new physical volume of "5.00 GiB"
    --- NEW Physical volume ---
    PV Name                /dev/sdb3
    VG Name
    PV Size                5.00 GiB
    Allocatable            NO
```

169

PE Size	0
Total PE	0
Free PE	0
Allocated PE	0
PV UUID	EQ7E1Z-WiGK-Z0m5-5gSN-gP95-MFSk-pKyTvS

2. Defining Volume Group (VG)

Once PV has been defined you can create VG over it. If more than one disk is used in creating VG then first create PVsfor all disks. Then use vgcreate command and all PV's name to define VG

vgcreate *VG_name PV_name or pv_names*

```
# vgcreate vg01 /dev/sdb3
  Volume group "vg01" successfully created
```

3. Create new Logical Volume(LV)

As mentioned LV is base for creating file system. LV can also be used as raw in some cases. To define LV use lvcreate command

```
lvcreate -n LV_name -L size VG_name
```

```
# lvcreate -n lv01 -L 1G vg01
  Logical volume "lv01" created
```

LV can be mirrored also. A mirror LV maintains identical copies of data on different devices. When data is written to one device, it is written to a second device as well for redundancy.

To create mirrored LV

```
# lvcreate -n lv01 -m1 -L 1G vg01
```

170

4. Create File System on LV

Use mkfs command to create filesystem

`mkfs -t xfs /dev/VG_name/LV_name`

where **-t** option is to specify the file system type and logical volume name is specified in hierarchical order with respect to it volume group

```
# mkfs -t xfs /dev/vg01/lv01
```

5. Make New File system mount automatically

To make file system mount automatically at system boot you have to add its entry in /etc/fstab file. There are two ways to do that first is to use device name other is device Universally Unique Identifier UUID. The advantage of using the UUID is that it is independent from the actual device number the operating system gives to your hard disk. Device name can change if you add new device, but device's UUID always remain same.

Add entry in fstab file with device name

vi /etc/fstab

```
/dev/sdb2   /newfs    xfs     defaults          1 2
```

Add entry in fstab file using UUID

1. Check the UUID of newly created file system

```
#  blkid /dev/vg01/lv01
```

2. Add entry to **/etc/fstab** mount system automatically at startup

```
UUID=6acaa-5541139e830e  /newfs    xfs     defaults       1 2
```

171

6. Mount the file system

```
mount -a
```

LVM Command Cheat sheet

PV Commands

Description	Command
Display PV properties	pvdisplay
Show all LVM block devices	pvscan
Prevent allocation of PE on PV	pvchange -xn */dev/PV_name*
Remove PV	pvremove */dev/PV_name*

Volume Group Commands

Description	Command
Display VG properties	vgdisplay
Display VG List	vgs
Add PV to VG	vgextend vgname */dev/PV_name* **Example** # vgextend vg01 /dev/sdb5
Remove PV from VG	vgreduce vg1 */dev/PV_name* **Example** # vgreduce vg01 /dev/sdb5
Activating VG	vgchange -ay *VG_name*
deactivating VG	vgchange -ay *VG_name*
Remove VG	vgremove *VG_name* **Example** vgremove /dev/vg02

Recreate a VG Directory	vgmknodes

Moving Volume group

If situation arises, in which you have to move whole volume group from one system to other system. It can be due to some hardware problem on the current system or for moving old storage to new hardware you can use following procedure. In this example, there are two systems one is old system on which VG is currently located and new system that is where you want to move.

On old system

1. Unmount all File systems which are part of Volume Group

```
umount /newfs
```

2. Deactivate the VG **vgchange -an *VG_name*** command

```
[root@RHEL1 /]# vgchange -an sharedvg
```

3. Export the VG with **vgexport *VG_name*** command

```
[root@RHEL1 /]# vgexport sharedvg
```

On the New System

4. After attaching HDD to new system, import the VG with `vgimport` `VG_name` command

```
[root@RHEL2 ~]# vgimport sharedvg
```

5. Activate the VG with **vgchange -ay VG_name**

```
[root@RHEL2 ~]# vgchange -ay sharedvg
```

173

6. Mount the file systems on the VG

```
[root@RHEL2 ~]# mount /dev/sharedvg/sharedlv /mnt
```

7. Check the contents of file system

```
[root@RHEL2 ~]# cd /mnt
```

Extending File System

1. Check the current FS size

```
df -h /fsname
```

```
/dev/mapper/vg01-lv01          1008M   34M  924M   4% /newfs
```

2. Check if you have enough free space i.e. free PE on the VG where LV of FS you want extend is there.

```
# vgdisplay vg01
  --- Volume group ---
  VG Name                vg01
  System ID
  Format                 lvm2
  Metadata Areas         1
  Metadata Sequence No   5
  VG Access              read/write
  VG Status              resizable
  MAX LV                 0
  Cur LV                 1
  Open LV                1
  Max PV                 0
  Cur PV                 1
  Act PV                 1
```

VG Size	5.00 GiB
PE Size	4.00 MiB
Total PE	1280
Alloc PE / Size	256 / 1.00 GiB
Free PE / Size	**1024 / 4.00 GiB**
VG UUID	EXKfhW-MfE4-4ZtU-uQuM-v9e4-AJ9k-Uo6z4B

3. Extend the Logical Volume `lvextend -L size /dev/vgname/lvname`

```
# lvextend -L +200M /dev/vg01/lv01
  Extending logical volume lv01 to 1.20 GiB
  Logical volume lv01 successfully resized
```

4. Extend the file system using

`xfs_growfs /fsname`

```
# xfs_growfs /newfs
```

5. Check the FS size

`df -h /fsname`

```
/dev/mapper/vg01-lv01        1.2G   34M  1.1G   3% /newfs
```

Reduce the File System

1. Check the current FS size

`df -h /fs_name`

```
/dev/mapper/vg01-lv01        1.2G   34M  1.1G   3% /newfs
```

2. Backup the File System

```
# xfsdump -f /tmp/newfs.dump /newfs
```

175

3. unmount the File system

```
umount /fs_name
```

```
# umount /newfs
```

4. Remove the LV

```
# lvremove /dev/mapper/vg01-lv01
```

5. Recreate LV

```
# lvcreate -n lv01 -L 1G vg01
```

6. Recreate the File system

```
# mkfs.xfs /dev/vg01/lv01
```

7. First check the UUID

```
# blkid /dev/vg01/lv01
```

8. Change the UUID of File system in /etc/fstab
9. Mount File System

```
# mount -a
```

10. Restore the backup

```
xfsrestore -f /tmp/newfs.dump /newfs
```

11. Check File System

```
# df -h /newfs
```

Chapter 21.

NFS

NFS (Network File System) is file sharing file system, which works on server client basis. Server's shared file systems are mounted on clients.

Four version of NFS are there:-

1.   NFS V1

2.   NFS V2

3.   NFS V3

4.   NFS V4

Where NFS V3 and NFS V4 are more recent version of NFS, V3 is safer and asynchronous works on UDP protocol while V4 has added advantage of working through firewall and works on TCP.

To make shared file system available on the client it has be exported from server. For exporting there are two ways to configure exports on an NFS server.

- Through `/etc/exports` configuration file.

- Explicitly Using the exportfs utility on the command line, but this way you have to do every time after reboot.

Configure NFS on the server

Install packages

```
# yum install nfs-utils
# yum install rpcbind
```

177

Start the services

```
# systemctl start rpcbind
# systemctl start nfs-server
```

Make service start on next reboot

```
# systemctl enable rpcbind
# systemctl enable nfs-server
```

To export file system without /etc/exports manually.

```
# exportfs -i /user1
```

To export file system using /etc/exports

Edit **/etc/exports** file to add file systems you want to share to clients

format of that is :-

```
mountpoint    [host][permissions/options]
```

where

mountpoint   is file systems you want export

host   is optional, the client you want to give access the
                 filesystems

permissions is optional it can be ro read only, rw read write insecure,

sync changes written before command finished.

Example

```
/software/c1      192.168.10.12(rw,sync)
```

Export file system

```
# exportfs -a
```

See the file system exported

```
# showmount -e
```

Configure firewall to allow NFS server to clients

```
firewall-cmd --permanent --zone public --add-service mountd
firewall-cmd --permanent --zone public --add-service rpc-bind
firewall-cmd --permanent --zone public --add-service nfs
firewall-cmd --reload
```

On client

```
# showmount -e server IP address / hostname
# mount -t nfs 192.168.0.1:/userfs /newmnt
```

To unexport all exported file system

```
# exportfs -ua
```

Chapter 22.

LVM snapshot

LVM snapshot is a point in time copy of Logical Volume. The snapshot provides static view of original volume. Once snapshot has been taken we can use this snapshot to take backup of volume as snapshot is static copy and it will not change while backup is happening unlike the original volume which is dynamic.

The snapshot volume size should be enough to store the data that will change after snapshot has been taken. The volume will store only changes after the snapshot has been taken.

Create snapshot LV

1. Check the LV name and size of File System for which you want to create snapshot

```
# df -hT /newfs
Filesystem          Type  Size  Used Avail Use% Mounted on
/dev/mapper/vg01-lv01 ext4 1008M   34M  924M   4% /newfs
```

2. Check you have space at least equivalent to 10% of file system you want to take snapshot available on the VG where original LV is located

```
# vgdisplay vg01
```

3. Create LV 8 to 10 % of capacity of original LV

```
lvcreate -s -n snaplvname -L size /dev/vgname/orginal_lv_name
```

```
# lvcreate -s -n snaplv1 -L 100M /dev/mapper/vg01-lv01
```

4. if you want to see content of snapshot LV

```
mount -o ro /dev/vgname/snaplv /mount_point_snaplv
```

```
# mount -o ro /dev/vg01/snaplv1 /snapfs/
```

5. Change to directory to check the contents

```
cd /mount_point_snaplv
```

```
# cd /snapfs/
# ls
```

Remove snapshot LV

Once you have taken backup and you do not want this snapshot, you can remove it using following procedure

1. Unmount snap File system

```
umount /mount_point_snaplv
```

```
[root@RHEL1 /]# umount /snapfs
```

2. Remove the snap logical volume

```
lvremove /dev/vgname/snaplv
```

```
[root@RHEL1 /]# lvremove /dev/mapper/vg01-snaplv1
```

Chapter 23.

Utilities and commands

In this chapter we will discuss some of the common command utilities very useful in RHEL administration. Most of the commands discussed in chapter can also be used on almost any flavor of Linux.

cp

Command to copy files

Syntax

```
cp <options> source destination
```

Example

```
cp /home/abc.txt /home1/
```

Copy all files in the directory recursively

```
cp -R /home/* /home1/
```

Prompt before any overwrite

```
cp -i /home /home1
```

Copy all new files to the destination

```
cp -u * /tmp
```

Forcefully copy files

```
cp -f /tmp/abc.txt /backup/.
```

Copy without prompting to overwrite

```
cp -n * t
```

scp

scp command is used to copy files from one host to another host in secured manner.

Copy files from local machine to remote machine

Syntax

```
scp filename remote_user@remote_host:/some/remote_diectory
```

Example

```
$ scp /home/ana/atom.txt adams@server1/home/adams/.
```

Copy files from remote host to local host

Syntax

```
scp remote_user@remote.host:/path/filename .
```

Example

```
$ scp adams@server1/home/adams/tasks.txt /home/ana/.
```

ls

Lists the names of Files

Syntax

```
ls -<options>
```

Example

```
$ ls -al              To list directories and files
```

cat

Displays a Text File

Syntax

```
cat filename
```

Example

```
$ cat abc.conf
```

rm

Deletes a file, files or directory

Syntax

```
rm filename
```

Example

```
rm abc.conf
```

To delete abc directory recursively

```
rm -r abc
```

more

When you want to view a file that is longer than one screen, you can use more utility. More is used for paging through text one screen full at a time.

Syntax

```
more filename
```

Example

```
more /etc/hosts
```

less

Less is a program similar to more, but it allows backward movement in the file as well as forward movement.

Syntax

```
less filename
```

Example

```
less /etc/hosts
```

mv

mv command is used to move file from one location to other location. mv command can also be used to rename the file.

mv command to move file

Syntax

```
mv filename destination_directory
```

Example

```
mv a.txt /tmp/.
```

It will move a.txt file from current directory to /tmp directory

To rename

Syntax

```
mv filename newfilename
```

Example

```
mv a.txt b.txt
```

grep

Searches for a String from one or more files. Display each line which has string.

Syntax

```
grep string file
```

Example

```
grep '127.0.0.1' /etc/hosts
```

head

Print the first 10 lines of file to standard output. You can also specify how many line it will show.

Syntax

```
head option file
```

Example

```
head -20 /tmp/abc.txt
```

This command will show first 20 lines of abc.txt file

tail

Print the last 10 lines of file to standard output if used without any parameter, otherwise you can specify number of lines to display.

Syntax

```
tail option file
```

Example

```
tail -20 /var/log/logfile
```

It will show last 20 lines

Use tail to monitor dynamic file continuously

```
tail -f /var/log/logfile
```

It will show end of growing file. Press Ctrl +c to interrupt.

diff

Compares two Files.

Syntax

```
diff First_file   Second_file
```

Example

```
diff abc.txt bbc.txt
```

file
Determine file type

Syntax

```
file file_name
```

Example

```
file bbc.txt
```

echo

Write arguments to the standard output

Syntax

```
echo text
```

Example

```
echo hello
```

date

Print or change the system data and time.

Syntax

```
date
```

Example

To check date

```
date
```

To set date and time

```
date -s "24 feb 2017 19:00"
```

Chapter 24.

Piping and Redirection

In the previous chapter we learned Linux commands in this chapter we will see how Linux commands and files can be used in conjunction with one another to turn simple commands into much more complex commands. This involves movement of data from one command to other command or command to file or file to command.

This data traveling from command to other command or file to command or command to file is known as stream. Stream can be of three types:-

•   Standard input (stdin)
•   Standard output (stdout)
•   Standard error (stderr)

Normally when user is working on a PC, standard input flows from keyboard of the user to standard out that is the monitor, where user gets the output. If there are errors in the operation the user will see the standard error on the terminal. However, we can change this behavior by using angle brackets and pipes. Some time we refer these streams with their corresponding numbers.

Stream	Number	Sign	Append
Stdin	0	<	<<
stdout	1	>	>>
stderr	2	2>	2>>

Redirection

When you want change the normal flow of data we use redirection. You can send output of the command to file or device. You can also take input from file or device to command.

Sending output to file (>)

Normally, we get our output on the screen, but if we wish to save it into a file, then greater than operator (>) is used to send the standard out to file. Please note this command will overwrite content of the existing output file.

Syntax

```
Command > filename
```

Example

```
ls > abc.txt
```

Sending input from file (<)

If we use the less than operator (<) then we can read data from file and feed it into the program via it's STDIN stream.

Syntax

```
Command < filename
```

Example

```
wc -l < abc.txt
```

Sending standard error to file

If we use 2 with greater than operator (2>) then we can send STDERR stream to a file.

Syntax

```
Command or script 2> filename
```

Example

```
myscript 2>abc.log
```

Append

We have seen that use of the single-bracket command overwrites the prior contents of the file. To append the content, we can use double brackets (>>) or (2>>)

To append the standard out to existing file or create new one if it is not there

Syntax

```
Command >> filename
```

Example

```
# la -la >> abc.txt
```

To append the stderr stream to file

Syntax

```
Command 2>> filename
```

Example

```
# myscript.sh 2>> abc.txt
```

Sometimes, you might want to redirect both standard output and standard error into same file. This is often done in case of automated processes so that you can later review the output and errors if any. Use &> or &>> to redirect both standard output and standard error to the same place. Another way is to use the numbers of the stream 2>&1

Syntax

```
Command >outputfile 2>&1
```

Example

```
ls b* >abc.log 2>&1
```

Piping (|)

For sending data from one program to another, we use pipe (|)

Syntax

```
Command1 | Command2
```

Example

```
ls | head -10
```

This command run the ls command and shows only first 10 lines of the output. This is simple example of pipe to explain, but you can use pipe for more complex use.

First sort the abc.txt and then use uniq command print unique values.

```
$ sort abc.txt | uniq
```

Chapter 25.

Process and threads

Every task done by Linux OS has process associated with it. A tasks may consist of one or more processes. In the simplest terms, process is an executing program. Further process is executed in form of threads. A thread is the basic unit to which the operating system allocates processor time. The idea is to achieve parallelism by dividing a process into multiple threads. The primary difference between process and thread is that threads within the same process run in a shared memory space, while processes run in separate memory spaces. Processes have following properties: -

- Process has priority based on the context switches on them.
- Each process provides required resources to execute the program.
- Each process starts with single thread known as primary thread.
- Process can have multiple threads.
- Process runs in foreground and background

Foreground Processes

A foreground process is any command or task you run directly and wait for it to complete.

Background Process

Background process are process which runs behind the scene. Unlike with a foreground process, the shell does not have to wait for a background process to end before it can run more processes. The maximum number of process that can run in background depends on amount of available memory.

Commands

Command	Description
bg	Sends job to Background
fg	Bring job to foreground
jobs	Show current jobs
kill	Stops the process
ps	Show the process information
&	if command ends with the & the shell execute the command in background and shell will not wait for finish Example `gcalctool &`

Bring command to foreground

```
$ fg
ctrl + c
```

Check the running jobs

```
$ jobs
```

List the current running process

```
$ ps -ef
```

or

```
$ ps aux
```

Kill the process forcefully

First check the process ID with **ps -ef** command then

```
$ sudo kill -9 <process -id >
```

Monitoring the process with ps command

ps command show the percentage of CPU & memory utilization of the process it is very useful if your machine is underperforming. ps command gives you indication which process is hogging memory/CPU.

Process scheduling

Scheduler is part of kernel, which select process to run next. The purpose is to run the processes according to priorities. To set the priority of running process nice and renice command is used which decide how longer or smaller CPU time is given to process.

Nice   set the priority or niceness of new process.

renice   adjust nice value of running process

niceness of -20 is highest priority and 19 is lowest priority. The default priority is 0

Example

```
$ sudo nice -n 19 cp -r /as /map
```

Commands show priorities of running processes

```
ps -al
```

or

```
top
```

195

To change the priority

```
$ sudo renice -n 10 <pid>
```

Note: You need root / superuser privilege to change to higher priority.

## Chapter 26

Automating tasks

Automation of task is very important in computer field. Suppose you have to take daily backup at 11.00 O'clock in the night when there is no usage of system. Then you have to come in night to take backup. However, you can schedule your backup then computer will run the backup script at 11.00 o'clock in night automatically. In the morning you can verify the backup. RHEL provides many utilities to automate the task. These utilities can be used to automate the tasks which system administrators do regularly or at specified time. Following are the main utilities

- cron
- at
- batch

cron

cron is daemon that can be used to schedule the execution of recurring tasks according to time, day of month, day of week.

Configuration file

/etc/crontab

Command	Description
crontab –l	List crontab entries
crontab –e	Edit crontab
crontab –r	Remove crontab

Format

minutes hours Day_of_month Month Day_of_week Command

Where

Minutes	(from 0 to 59)
hours	(from 0 to 23)
day of month	(from 1 to 31)
month	(from 1 to 12)
day of week	(from 0 to 6) (0=Sunday)

To schedule a recurring task

1. Edit crontab by giving command **crontab -e**

2. Add entries at bottom of file press **i** (Note this files will open in vi editor so you can use all vi commands)

Suppose you want to run backup script every night at 11:30

```
30     23 * * *      /myscripts/backup.sh
```

3. Press **ESCAPE** and press : write **x** after that press **ENTER** to save the entry .

at and batch

crontab is used for recurring task but for one time tasks at specified time at and batch commands can be used.

To run **at** command rpm must be installed and **atd** service must be running. When you give at command with time, the system presents you the at prompt. On at prompt you can give the commands you want to schedule. After giving all commands, you press **CTRL + d** key to exit from at prompt.

Check Installation

```
# rpm -q at
```

Install at package

```
# yum install at
```

Start service

```
# service start atd
```

Start command

```
# at 4:00
at > ls
ctrl + d
```

Batch command executes one-time task when system average load decreases bellow 0.8

```
~]# batch
at> ls -la
at> ctrl + d
```

Display list of pending jobs

```
# atq
```

Chapter 27.

Boot process

After pressing power on button to RHEL login prompt screen, system do lot of processing to get you to login prompt. This process is known as boot process. It is important to understand the boot process of Linux to troubleshoot startup issues and to configure Linux properly.

The following steps summarize how the boot procedure happens in RHEL

1. Computer uses **BIOS** to perform POST.

2. BIOS reads **Master Boot Record** for bootloader.

3. Control goes to **GRUB2**. It uses /boot/grub/grub.cfg to select the kernel image.

4. **Kernel**

   1. Mounts the **root filesystem** as specified with "root=" in grub.conf

   2. The kernel starts the **systemd** process with a process ID of 1 (PID 1)

   3. **initrd** which stands for Initial RAM Disk is used by kernel as temporary root file system until kernel is booted and the real root filesystem is mounted. It also contains drivers, which are required to access hard disk and other necessary hardware.

5. **systemd**

   Systemd is a system and service manager for Linux operating systems. Provides a number of features such as parallel startup of system services at boot time. systemd is the parent process of all processes on a system. systemd determine the default system target earlier it used to be known as run level in older version. After determining the target, it performs the initialization of system, which includes

1. Setting the host name
2. Initializing the network
3. Initializing the system hardware
4. Mounting the file systems
5. Starting swapping

Chapter 28.

Log management

Log files are very useful in troubleshooting the system. Log files are also useful in auditing system for unauthorized system access. Log files give you an idea that what system was doing at specific point in time. Suppose your machine is running slow or not working properly as a Linux administrator, first thing to look for problem is logs. Logs provides clue when and how problem started and what part of OS is giving problem.

The log files generated in a Linux environment can normally be classified into four different categories:

- Application Logs
- Event Logs
- Service Logs
- System Logs

RHEL provide services for saving log information. Some application in RHEL use their own mechanism to logs directly to their log information files, example of which is apache Some of the service maintain their logs through systemctl. systemctl further communicates to Journald which keep track on log information.

rsyslog is another logging method. rsyslog and Journal, have several distinguishing features that make them suitable for specific use cases. In many situations, it is useful to combine their capabilities.

journald

journald daemon is a component of systemd which is used for logs management. It's a centralized location for all messages logged by different components in a systemd enabled Linux system. This includes kernel and boot messages, initial RAM disk, messages coming from syslog or different services, it indexes and makes them available to the user. Log data collected by the journal is primarily text-based but can also include binary data where necessary. Log files produced by journald are not persistent, log files are stored only in memory or a small ring-buffer in the /run/log/journal/ directory. The amount of logged data depends on free memory. Logs gets rotated periodically. But you can configure the system to make these logs persistent.

Viewing log with journalctl

To view log

```
journalctl
```

To view full meta data about all entries

```
journalctl -o verbose
```

Live view of logs

```
journalctl -f
```

Filtering by Priority

You can filter the logs on basis of priority.

Syntax

```
journalctl -p priority
```

Example

In this example, we want to view only lines with error from the log

```
journalctl -p err
```

To view log entries only from the current boot

```
journalctl -b
```

To make logs persistent

```
$ sudo mkdir -p /var/log/journal
```

Then, restart journald to apply the change:

```
systemctl restart systemd-journald
```

Rsyslogd

Some logs are controlled by rsyslogd daemon. It is enhanced replacement of sysklogd. It offers high-performance, great security features, modular design and support for transportation via the TCP or UDP protocols. Every logged message contains at least a time and normally a program name field.

/etc/rsyslog.conf

The rsyslog.conf file is the main configuration file for the rsyslogd which logs system messages on the systems. This file specifies rules for logging rsyslogd. List of log files maintained by rsyslogd can be found in the rsyslog.conf configuration file. Log files are usually located in the /var/log/ directory.

Sample rsyslog.conf

```
etc]$ cat rsyslog.conf
# rsyslog v5 configuration file
```

```
# For more information see /usr/share/doc/rsyslog-
*/rsyslog_conf.html
# If you experience problems, see
http://www.rsyslog.com/doc/troubleshoot.html


*.info;mail.none;authpriv.none;cron.none
/var/log/messages


# The authpriv file has restricted access.
authpriv.*
/var/log/secure


# Log all the mail messages in one place.
mail.*                                                    -
/var/log/maillog



# Log cron stuff
cron.*
/var/log/cron


# Everybody gets emergency messages
*.emerg                                                   *


# Save news errors of level crit and higher in a special file.
uucp,news.crit
/var/log/spooler


# Save boot messages also to boot.log
local7.*
/var/log/boot.log
```

Log filtering with rsyslog.conf

There is too much logging happens in the system, if it is not filtered it becomes almost impossible to use these logs. To filter the logs, we use /etc/rsyslog.conf file. It has two parameter facility and priority separated with dot (.). Facility is name of process for which you want to log and priority specify level of log like debug, info, notice, warning, err, crit, alert, emerg or * for all type of messages you want to keep.

Example

```
# The authpriv file has restricted access.
authpriv.*
/var/log/secure

# Log all the mail messages in one place.
mail.*                                        -
/var/log/maillog
```

In the example where authpriv and mail is facility and priority is * which means all logs.

Rotating logs with logrotate

Logs needs rotation to avoid filling of file systems and make log more manageable. Once log file is rotated, it will be renamed with new file name. After certain time of rotation, older log files are deleted to save space.

logrotate package manages automatic rotation of log files according to configuration in **/etc/logrotate.conf** or otherwise specified with command option

Install

```
sudo apt install logrotate
```

To verify if logrotate installed successfully

```
logrotate
```

Some of the important configuration settings in /etc/logrotate.conf file are rotation-interval, log-file-size, permssions of files, missingok, rotation-count and compression. For each log it is recommended you create file in the **/etc/logrotate.d** directory

Example

```
[root@redhat1 logrotate.d]# cat bootlog
/var/log/boot.log
{
    missingok
    daily
    copytruncate
    rotate 7
    notifempty
}
```

In this example the log rotation utility rotate the logs for boot with following details :-

Missingok	ignore if logs are missing
Daily	log is rotated on daily.
copytruncate	Truncate the original log file in place after creating a copy
rotate 7	retain logs for 7 days.
notifempty	Do not rotate the log if it is empty

Important logs

The main directory for logs is /var/log . Some of the important log files in this directory is worth mentioning

- wtmp
- utmp
- dmesg
- messages
- maillog
- spooler
- auth.log or secure
- yum.log
- boot.log

/var/log/wtmp and /var/run/utmp

The wtmp and utmp files keep track of users logging in and out of the system. These two files are binary files. You cannot directly read the contents of these files using text editor, cat or more command. You have to use specific command for that.

who command uses /var/run/utmp file to provide information about the users who are currently logged onto the system.

```
[root@RHEL2 log]# who
(unknown) :0          2018-10-02 05:34 (:0)
root      pts/0       2018-10-02 05:38 (192.168.131.1)
```

/var/log/wtmp file

This file maintains history of all logged in and logged out users. The **last** command uses this file to display listing of last logged in users.

```
[root@RHEL2 log]# last
```

```
root       pts/0           192.168.131.1      Tue Oct  2 05:38    still logged in
(unknown :0               :0                  Tue Oct  2 05:34    still logged in
reboot    system boot   3.10.0-514.el7.x Tue Oct  2 05:33 - 05:47   (00:13)
root       pts/1           192.168.131.1      Mon Oct  1 13:23 - crash  (16:10)
root       pts/0           :0                  Mon Oct  1 13:21 - 13:35  (00:14)
root       :0              :0                  Mon Oct  1 13:20 - 13:35  (00:15)
----output truncated---
```

dmesg

dmesg obtains its data by reading the kernel ring buffer. A buffer is a portion of a computer's memory that is set aside as a temporary holding place for data that is being sent to or received from an external device. The messages are very important in terms of diagnosing purpose in case of device failure. Whenever there is hardware change happens most the time messages are logged here. If you are facing any problem, use dmesg for system diagnosis. dmesg tool uses dmesg file present in /var/log/ directory

```
[root@RHEL2 log]# dmesg |more
[    0.000000] Initializing cgroup subsys cpuset
[    0.000000] Initializing cgroup subsys cpu
[    0.000000] Initializing cgroup subsys cpuacct
[    0.000000] Linux version 3.10.0-514.el7.x86_64
(builder@kbuilder.dev.RHEL.org) (gcc version 4.8.5 20150623 (Red Hat 4.8.5-
11) (GCC) ) #1 SMP Tue Nov 22 16:42:41 U
TC 2016
[    0.000000] Command line: BOOT_IMAGE=/boot/vmlinuz-3.10.0-514.el7.x86_64
root=UUID=07547f5a-9e65-45a4-ab2d-2e8bb48bef3a ro crashkernel=auto rhgb quiet
LANG=en_US.UTF
---- output truncated---
```

Messages

General messages are logged in this file. To view this file, you can use text editor or any common tool for viewing text file like cat, less or more.

Example

```
[root@RHEL2 log]# cat messages
Oct  2 06:07:02 localhost rsyslogd: [origin software="rsyslogd"
swVersion="7.4.7" x-pid="1056" x-info="http://www.rsyslog.com"]
rsyslogd was HUPed
Oct  2 06:10:02 localhost systemd: Started Session 6 of user root.
Oct  2 06:10:02 localhost systemd: Starting Session 6 of user root.
Oct  2 06:20:01 localhost systemd: Started Session 7 of user root.
```

Maillog

This file logs the messages for mail server running on the server.

Example

```
[root@RHEL2 log]# cat maillog
Feb 25 16:26:24 RHEL1 postfix/postfix-script[1371]: starting the Postfix mail system
Feb 25 16:26:24 RHEL1 postfix/master[1379]: daemon started -- version 2.10.1,
configuration /etc/postfix
Feb 26 01:57:23 RHEL1 postfix/postfix-script[1980]: starting the Postfix mail system
Feb 26 01:57:24 RHEL1 postfix/master[2045]: daemon started -- version 2.10.1,
configuration /etc/postfix
Feb 26 23:43:36 RHEL1 postfix/postfix-script[1591]: starting the Postfix mail system
Feb 26 23:43:36 RHEL1 postfix/master[1641]: daemon started -- version 2.10.1,
configuration /etc/postfix
Feb 27 03:07:58 RHEL1 postfix/postfix-script[1670]: starting the Postfix mail system
Feb 27 03:07:58 RHEL1 postfix/master[1764]: daemon started -- version 2.10.1,
configuration /etc/postfix
Feb 27 18:13:22 RHEL1 postfix/postfix-script[1494]: starting the Postfix mail system
```

Spooler

Logs the spooler messages. Spooler is used by print queues to print.

secure

This file captures authentication logs. To check this file, you can use more
or less command.

dnf.log

As in RHEL 8 yum is frontend for dnf command Yum command logs messages in dnf.log file. There are other dnf log files like dnf.librepo.log and dnf.rpm.log

Example

```
[root@redhat1 log]# cat dnf.log
2019-11-20T21:46:42Z INFO --- logging initialized ---
2019-11-20T21:46:42Z DDEBUG timer: config: 11 ms
2019-11-20T21:46:42Z DEBUG Loaded plugins: builddep, changelog,
config-manager, copr, debug, debuginfo-install, download,
generate_completion_cache, needs-restarting, playground, product-id,
repoclosure, repodiff, repograph, repomanage, reposync, subscription-
manager, uploadprofile
-- output truncated ---
```

Boot.log

Contains information that are logged when the system boots.

```
[root@RHEL2 log]# cat boot.log
[  OK  ] Started Show Plymouth Boot Screen.
[  OK  ] Reached target Paths.
[  OK  ] Reached target Basic System.
[  OK  ] Found device VMware_Virtual_S 1.
         Starting File System Check on /dev/disk/by-
uuid/07547f5a-9e65-45a4-ab2d-2e8bb48bef3a...
[  OK  ] Started File System Check on /dev/disk/by-
uuid/07547f5a-9e65-45a4-ab2d-2e8bb48bef3a.
[  OK  ] Started dracut initqueue hook.
[  OK  ] Reached target Remote File Systems (Pre).
[  OK  ] Reached target Remote File Systems.
--- Output truncated -----------
```

These are the few log files we discussed, there are more files in the /var/log directory you can go through these files to know more about them.

Chapter 29.

Selinux

Selinux is **Security Enhanced Linux**. Selinux is kernel module that improves the Linux server security. This is one of the solution for implementation of Access Control in Linux.

Selinux implements MAC, Mandatory Access Control. Selinux is set of security rules, which determine which process can access which file, directory or port etc. Selinux policy to access process, directory, and files is known as context. One goal of Selinux is to protect data and system. Selinux has three forms of access control:

1.   Enforcing
2.   Permissive
3.   Disabled

Enforcing
Selinux denies access based on SELinux policy rules.

Permissive
Selinux does not deny access but denials are logged for the action that would have been denied if running in enforcing mode.

Disabled
Selinux is completely disabled

Check the installation

```
# rpm -qa | grep selinux
```

Install selinux

```
# yum install policycoreutils policycoreutils-python
```

Check current mode

```
# getenforce
```

Check the status

```
# sestatus
```

Main configuration file

/etc/selinux/config

To Change the mode

Edit /etc/Selinux/config configuration file and change selinux=enforcing to desired mode like selinux= permissive. After saving the file and reboot the server.

If you set the mode to permissive, you can check the log to see what Selinux is doing.

```
# cat /var/log/messages |grep -i selinux
```

Or

```
tail -f /var/log/audit/audit.log
```

Commands to display context

Description	Command
List process conext	ps auxZ
Display user context	Id –Z
Display files with context	ls -lZ
copy with context	cp -Z
mkdir with context	mkdir -Z

Tool to change context

```
# semanage
```

Show context

```
# semanage fcontext -1
```

Types

The main permission control method used in SELinux targeted policy to provide advanced process isolation is Type Enforceing. All files and processes are labeled as a type. Types define a SELinux domain for processes and a SELinux type for files

Example of Types are

httpd_sys_content_t

tmp_t

Add context

```
# semanage fcontext -a -t httpd_sys_content_t  /abc/zzz.txt
# ls -Z
-rw-r--r--. root root unconfined_u:object_r:samba_share_t:s0
zzz.txt
```

215

Set the context to default

```
# restorecon -v -t /abc/zzz.txt
```

Booleans

Booleans allow a part of Selinux policy to change at runtime without any knowledge of Selinux policy writing

List Booleans

```
# semanage boolean -l
```

Configure Booleans

In this example, we will allow ftp read and write access in user's home directory

1. list all

```
semanage boolean -l
```

2. list Booleans weather they are on/off

```
getsebool -a
```

3. Allow ftp read and write files in the user's home directory

```
setsebool -P ftp_home_dir on
```

4. Check

```
# getsebool ftp_home_dir
ftp_home_dir --> on
```

## Chapter 30

System Monitoring Tools

Continues monitoring is vital part of the system administration. System monitoring helps in properly provision resources for your projects. It also helps in fine tuning the server. Monitoring helps in avoiding the unnecessary down time due to resource bottleneck as proper monitoring you can add the required hardware before it leads to server crash or denial of service. Sometime monitoring helps in predicting the hardware failure for example you can use smart tools to predict hard disk failure.

Viewing system processes

ps

Display report of running process. It is a snapshot of the current processes at time of running command.

To see every process on the system and their owner

```
ps aux
```

To list all related threads after each process

```
ps axms
```

Top

top command displays processor activity of Linux machine The top command displays list of running processes on the system It also displays additional information about current usage of CPU, memory and swap space.

```
# top

top - 21:59:05 up  5:58,  3 users,  load average: 0.16, 0.03, 0.01
Tasks: 188 total,   1 running, 187 sleeping,   0 stopped,   0 zombie
%Cpu(s):  0.0 us,  0.7 sy,  0.0 ni, 97.7 id,  1.0 wa, 0.3 hi,  0.3 si, 0.0 st
KiB Mem :  2045748 total,   168512 free,  1038120 used,   839116 buff/cache
KiB Swap:  2097148 total,  1906704 free,   190444 used.   891936 avail Mem


   PID USER      PR  NI    VIRT    RES    SHR S %CPU %MEM     TIME+ COMMAND
  1771 root      20   0  406112  10888   7084 S  0.3  0.5   0:30.40 vmtoolsd
  5854 root      20   0  156652   3960   3456 R  0.3  0.2   0:00.03 top
     1 root      20   0  215220   8316   5820 S  0.0  0.4   0:09.58 systemd
     2 root      20   0       0      0      0 S  0.0  0.0   0:00.03 kthreadd
     3 root      20   0       0      0      0 S  0.0  0.0   0:02.07
--- Output truncated ---
```

System Monitor Tool

System monitor tool is GUI tool for system monitoring. The Processes
tab allows you to view, search for, change the priority of, and kill
processes. Press Activities   > Write **System monitor** in search bar.
Click **Processes** tab to view the list of running processes.

Process Name	User	% CPU	ID	Memory	Disk read tota	Disk write tot	Disk read	Disk write	Priority
alsactl	root	0	931	144.0 KiB	N/A	N/A	N/A	N/A	Very Low
ata_sff	root	0	432	N/A	N/A	N/A	N/A	N/A	Very High
atd	root	0	1486	204.0 KiB	56.0 KiB	N/A	N/A	N/A	Normal
at-spi2-registryd	root	0	7786	788.0 KiB	N/A	N/A	N/A	N/A	Normal
at-spi-bus-launcher	root	0	7778	748.0 KiB	N/A	N/A	N/A	N/A	Normal
auditd	root	0	894	604.0 KiB	140.0 KiB	108.0 KiB	N/A	N/A	High
bash	root	0	8147	1.7 MiB	488.0 KiB	N/A	N/A	N/A	Normal
bash	root	0	8348	1.7 MiB	16.6 MiB	11.1 MiB	N/A	N/A	Normal
bluetoothd	root	0	928	484.0 KiB	1.1 MiB	N/A	N/A	N/A	Normal
boltd	root	0	2251	780.0 KiB	172.0 KiB	N/A	N/A	N/A	Normal
cpuhp/0	root	0	13	N/A	N/A	N/A	N/A	N/A	Normal
crond	root	0	1481	880.0 KiB	232.0 KiB	N/A	N/A	N/A	Normal
crypto	root	0	24	N/A	N/A	N/A	N/A	N/A	Very High
cupsd	root	0	1047	1.4 MiB	1.5 MiB	8.0 KiB	N/A	N/A	Normal
dbus-daemon	root	0	1592	1.4 MiB	428.0 KiB	N/A	N/A	N/A	Normal
dbus-daemon	root	0	7783	496.0 KiB	N/A	N/A	N/A	N/A	Normal
dconf-service	root	0	7827	628.0 KiB	100.0 KiB	64.0 KiB	N/A	N/A	Normal
dm_bufio_cache	root	0	9020	N/A	N/A	N/A	N/A	N/A	Very High

To kill the process right click on the process and select the operation
like kill the selected process.

Process Name		User	% CPU	ID	Memory	Disk
accounts-daemon		root	0	1008	944.0 KiB	3
acpi_thermal_pm		root	0	122	N/A	
alsactl		root	0	931	144.0 KiB	
ata_sff		root	0	432	N/A	
atd			0	1486	204.0 KiB	
at-?	Properties Alt+Return		0	7786	788.0 KiB	
at-?	Memory Maps Ctrl+M		0	7778	748.0 KiB	
aud	Open Files Ctrl+O		0	894	604.0 KiB	1
bas	Change Priority ▶		0	8147	1.7 MiB	4
bas	Stop Ctrl+S		0	8348	1.7 MiB	:
blu	Continue Ctrl+C		0	928	484.0 KiB	
bol	End Ctrl+E		0	2251	780.0 KiB	1
cpu	Kill Ctrl+K		0	13	N/A	
crond		root	0	1481	880.0 KiB	2

Processes | Resources

Click resources tab to check CPU, memory and Swap space utilization. It also shows network activities.

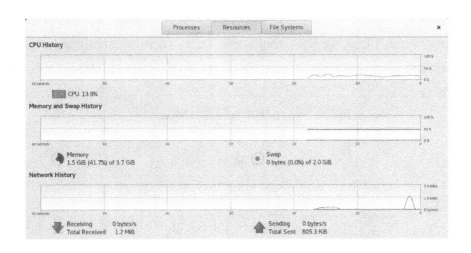

219

File system tab provide information about filesystem type, total size, available, used and percentage used.

Free

Free command provides information about system memory and swap space

```
~]# free
              total      used      free    shared  buff/cache    available
Mem:        2045748   1066888    135120      7596      843740        863048
Swap:       2097148    193704   1903444
```

To view memory in Megabytes

```
# free -m
```

lsblk

The lsblk command displays information about available block devices which includes block device's major and minor number, size, type and mount point.

```
~]# lsblk -a
NAME            MAJ:MIN RM   SIZE RO TYPE MOUNTPOINT
sda               8:0    0    20G  0 disk
├─sda1            8:1    0     1G  0 part /boot
└─sda2            8:2    0  17.9G  0 part
  ├─cl-root     253:0    0  15.9G  0 lvm  /
  └─cl-swap     253:1    0     2G  0 lvm  [SWAP]
```

blkid

To get UUID of a block device

```
~]# blkid /dev/sda1
/dev/sda1: UUID="b4bd5914a11" TYPE="ext4" PARTUUID="f2f7d4-01"
```

Partx

The partx command display a list of disk partitions.

To display list of partition for a device

```
~]# partx -s /dev/sda
NR   START       END  SECTORS SIZE NAME UUID
 1    2048   2099199  2097152   1G       f2acf7d4-01
 2 2099200  41943039 39843840  19G       f2acf7d4-02
```

findmnt

The findmnt command allows you to list all mounted file systems

```
~]# findmnt
TARGET    SOURCE              FSTYPE         OPTIONS
/         /dev/mapper/cl-root xfs   rw,relatime,seclabel
├─/sys    sysfs        sysfs         rw,nosuid,nodev,noexec,r|
---Output truncated to fit in window-----
```

du

The du command allows you to display disk usage by files in a directory

```
~]# du
4        ./Templates
4        ./Music
4        ./.pki/nssdb
8        ./.pki
24       ./.gnupg
```

221

To display output in human readable format i.e. the size in KB and MB

```
~]# du -h
4.0K     ./Templates
4.0K     ./Music
4.0K     ./.pki/nssdb
8.0K     ./.pki
24K      ./.gnupg
```

Display summary

```
~]# du -sh
9.1M    .
```

df

The df command displays report of file system disk space usage.

To display the disk space usage by each file system

```
~]# df -h
Filesystem              Size  Used  Avail Use% Mounted on
devtmpfs                476M     0   476M   0% /dev
tmpfs                   487M  336K   487M   1% /dev/shm
tmpfs                   487M  2.4M   485M   1% /run
--Output Truncated ---
```

Chapter 31.

Cockpit

In redhat 8 one of the prominent addition is web console known as cockpit. In Redhat version 8 it is available in main repositories and firewall is already opened for Cockpit. Cockpit is a web based interface designed for managing and monitoring Redhat system locally or anywhere on the network. Cockpit also allows to manage multiple servers Although cockpit was available since long time but it was made available in main repositories in RHEL 8. It makes possible to perform system tasks with a mouse. Following tasks can be achieved with cockpit:-

- System performance overview and live performance graphs
- Logs
- Managing storage
- Managing user accounts
- Managing services
- Configuring network interfaces and firewall
- Create Diagnostic report
- Kdump Configuration
- SELinux
- Software updates
- Subscription
- Terminal
- Managing virtual machines

Installing Cockpit

If Cockpit is not installed by default you can install with following procedure

Install

```
# yum install cockpit
```

Start the service

```
# systemctl start cockpit
```

Enable the service to start on boot

```
# systemctl enable cockpit
```

Check weather service is running or not

```
# systemctl status cockpit.socket
```

Firewall is by default opened for cockpit in RHEL 8 if it is not there you can do with following command

```
# firewall-cmd --add-service=cockpit --permanent
# firewall-cmd --reload
```

Starting the web console (cockpit)

You can start cockpit on the same server in the firefox browser, if GUI is installed. On MS Windows client you can use web browser of your choice.

The default https port for cockpit is 9090 and username and password is same as system credentials.

In this example I am running cockpit from windows 10 workstation the IP Address of the server 192.168.190.128. So in the address bar of the

browser like chrome or Microsoft internet explorer write
https://192.168.190.190:9090 . if you are running on same server write
https://localhost:9090 in address bar of the browser and press enter.

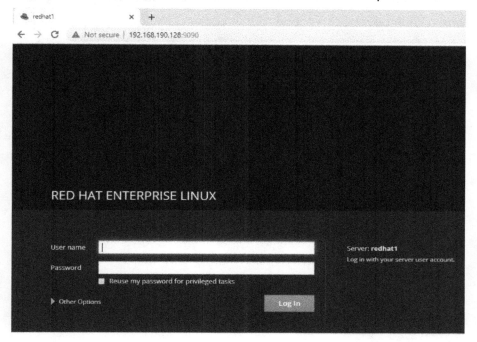

Installing add-ons

To add the add-on modules to cockpit

Syntax

```
# yum install package
```

Example

```
# yum install cockpit-machines
```

To manage multiple machines in single UI you can install dashboard
package

```
# yum install cockpit-dashboard
```

Exploring Cockpit

In this section I will do few task as a demonstration, going through the whole UI is beyond the scope of this book.

Shutdown / Restart the server

To shutdown or restart the machine using cockpit :-

From the left hand side pan select System > Power options

Under Power options drop down menu select the task whether you want to Restart or Shutdown the server.

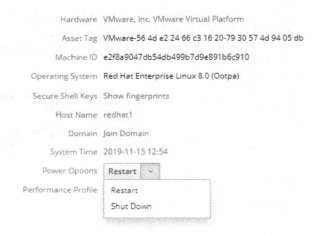

On next screen specify when you want to shutdown/restart the machine and message you want to send the message to logged in users .

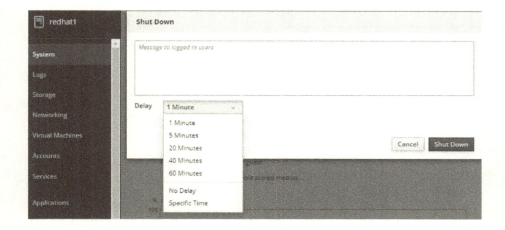

Set the hostname

Click host name on the system screen

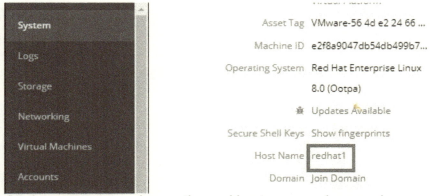

On the next screen change the real hostname and press change

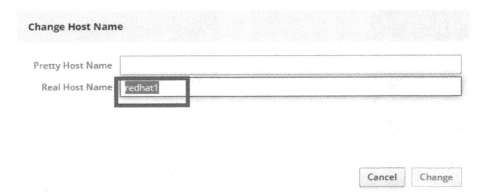

These are few example of task that can be performed with cockpit. As it is GUI you can explore and learn more.